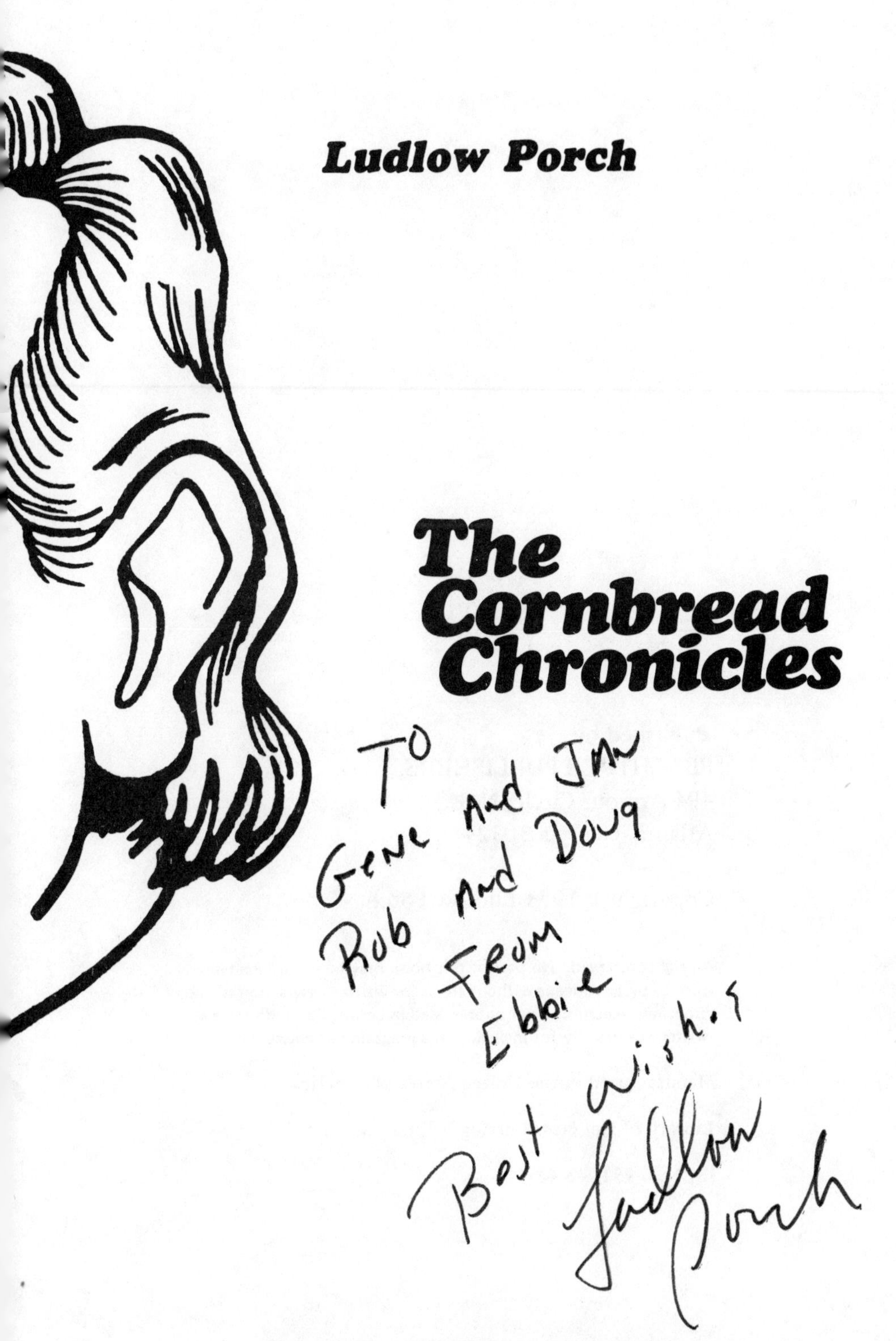

Ludlow Porch

The Cornbread Chronicles

TO
Gene and Jan
Rob and Doug
FROM
Ebbie

Best wishes
Ludlow Porch

Peachtree Publishers Limited

Published by
PEACHTREE PUBLISHERS, LTD.
494 Armour Circle, N. E.
Atlanta, Georgia 30324

Manufactured in the United States of America

Library of Congress Catalog Number 83-61914

ISBN: 0-931948-48-7

Dedication

When you love a woman like I love Diane, it's almost impossible to describe the way you feel.

She surrounds me with happiness. She makes our home a sanctuary that is full of all the good things of life. She fills my life with laughter.

Sometimes, when I think about how much I love her and what she means to me, tears come to my eyes and I feel inadequate and unworthy. How, on God's earth, can anyone give so much and ask for so little? She amazes me everyday with all the little ways she says, "I love you." She says it with king-sized towels always ready after my shower. She says it when she laughs at a speech that she's heard a thousand times. She says it when she pretends to agree that the Cadillac I just bought was a necessity; she knew I wanted it, and that was enough for her. She says it when she wears my favorite perfume. She says it when she sits in the cold and rain, with me, watching a football game that she has no interest in. She says it when she bought me the horse that I had always dreamed of owning; how do you thank someone for making a dream come true? She says it every time she touches me, or comes into a room, or holds my hand.

Irving Berlin said it far better than I could when he wrote, "The girl that I marry will have to be soft and pink as a nursery. The girl I call my own will wear satins and laces, and smell of cologne. A doll I can carry, the girl that I marry must be."

She has every quality that you could ask for in a best friend and a wife. I enjoy her company more than anyone else's I've ever known.

It took me half a lifetime to find her, but it was worth the search. I couldn't make it twenty-four hours without her.

I don't guess anyone on earth is perfect, but she comes close. I pray that I live long enough and settle down enough to someday be worthy of her.

Also by Ludlow Porch:

A View From the Porch

Acknowledgements

Special thanks go to my Diane, for the recipes in this book, and for more things than I could get into ten books;

To my beloved Aunt Kat, for typing this manuscript, and for a lifetime of her love and friendship;

To King Cotton, for suggesting the title;

To Bill Vale, for his warm friendship, and for making me sound more professional than I am;

To David Bowman, and the wonderful people at the Dictaphone Corporation, for making the writing of this book much easier;

To Marlene Sanders, for typing the recipes, and for letting me beat her in arm wrestling;

To Ron Jenkins, for being my best friend in good times and bad;

To the great cooks who shared their recipes and experience — Teenie Gillespi, Barbara Cox, Judy Merritt, Dave (Boo-Boo) deGraauw, Sue Tomlinson, and Paul Sachetti, who, along with Jimmy Watson, owns and operates Hennessy's Restaurant, where the top line on the menu is always hospitality;

And to Skip Caray, who gave me twenty-five dollars to put his name in this book.

Contents

That Old Gang of Mine

The Bigger They Are . . . 3
Ancestors 4
Buffy's Tattoo Garden 5
Baptism Under Fire 6
Country Titles 7
Self-Defense 9
Willard's Wonder Wieners 10
Granny's Curses 11
Black Cord Fever 12
A Funny Man 13
Floyd's News Conference 15
Aging Gracefully 17
A Sure Bet 18
Salesman Supreme 19
Reincarnation 21
I Cannot Tell a Lie 22
Rotunda Johnson 23
Real Class 24
Sexaholics Anonymous 25
The Conversation 26
The Château Switchblade 28
Exchanging Vows — and Blows 29
Discipline in School 31
My Bird Dog 32
I'm Whacko, by Doc of Birmingham 33
Land of Opportunity 34
The Psychiatrist 35

English Is a Foreign Language

Changing Meanings 39
Stupid Questions 41
Pebbles and Pops 42
Gimme a What? 43
Chortling 44
Language Barrier 45
Strange Things 46
A Brand-New Word 47
What's Your Phobia? 48
The Name Game 49
Taking Orders 50
Metric Nonsense 51
Wise Old Sayings 52

Those Days of Yore

The Service Station 55
The Old Comics 56
Sissies 57
That Old Magic 58
Convenience Stores 59
The Carnival 60
Video Games 61
WWII Memories 62
Rich Things 63
A Dying Memory 64
So Long, Joe 65
Good Old Days 66
Where Are You, Rula Lenska? 67
Double Bubble 68

Take It from Ludlow . . .

Bad Days 71
Non-Status Seekers 73
Never Do These Things 74
Painless Suicide? 76
Things I'd Like to See 77
Vacations 79
Health Test 80
Buying a House 81
You've Had Enough 82
Barbecue Standards 83
Child Psychology 84
Despicable Things 85
The Truth Hurts 86
Crime Signals 88

Contemplations, Condemnations, and Consolations

Stray Dogs 91
Prison Rights 92
Possums 93
Cocaine 94
Southern Limitations 95
The Water Department 96
The American Pie 98
Raiding Party 99
Wolves for Gun Control 100
The Dummies 101
What Do You See, Nurses? 102
Heartaches 104
Chain Letters 105

Hide-and-Seek **106**
Put It Off Till Tomorrow **107**
Things I Don't Understand **108**
Once Moor, With Feeling **109**
No Children **110**
New Car Fever **111**
Job Opportunity **112**
My New Telephone **113**
Grounded **114**
Sex Discrimination **115**
Did You Notice? **117**
Canadian Rats **118**
It's Bad for You **119**
The House We Live In **120**

Television, Rock Music, and Other Wastelands

The New Soap Operas **125**
Comic Capers **127**
Headlines **128**
Scripts Have Changed **129**
Radio Appreciation **130**
Spring Is Sprung **131**
Hairy Commercials **132**
Gird Your Loins **133**
Silver Screen Injustice **134**
Music Review **135**
Good Guys and Bad Guys **136**
Surviving the Eighties **137**
Confusing Commercials **138**
Rock-a-Bye **139**

Commercial Education **140**
Off-Color Country **141**
Bulldog Drummond Could Have Whipped Billie Jack **142**

Food—the Forbidden Fruit

White Bread — Long May She Wave **147**
Fancy Lunches **148**
Diet Foods **149**
Ode to Bread **150**
Wonderful Grits **151**
Those Little Onion Sandwiches **152**
While We Slept **154**
Recipes
- Ludlow's Recipe for Sunday Brunch **155**
- Cornbread **158**
- Easy Chili **159**
- Hurry-Up Breakfast **160**
- Liver and Onions **161**
- Pimento Cheese **162**
- Irish Coffee **163**
- Sue's Little Chicken Sandwiches **164**
- Vichyssoise **165**
- Boo-Boo's Creole Red Beans and Rice **166**
- Broccoli Casserole **167**
- Boo-Boo's Cajun Seafood Gumbo **168**
- Chicken Salad **170**
- Cocktail Meatballs **171**
- Ludlow's Favorite Potato Recipe **172**
- Mother's Smothered Chicken **173**
- Shrimp Salad **174**

Strawberry Pie **175**
Spaghetti Sauce **176**
Spinach-Artichoke Business **177**
Best Friend Chicken Casserole **178**
Milky Way Cake **179**
Chocolate-Marshmallow Frosting **180**
Aunt Barbara's Rice **181**
Aunt Teenie's Pepper Relish **182**

Trivial Trivia

Ludlow's Trivia Quiz **185**
Answers to Ludlow's Trivia Quiz **187**

That Old Gang of Mine

The Bigger They Are . . .

My old friend Basil is what we, down South, call wiry. Now, when you say somebody is wiry, what you mean is that they are little, skinny, and slightly on the wormy side. You refer to them as wiry so you don't hurt their feelings.

While my friend Basil was little and skinny and slightly wormy, he did have a fighting heart. One day when Basil was about sixteen, he caught his girl Roxie talking to the star tackle of the football team, an ole boy named Gorilla Gibson. Basil was real jealous, so he ran up and hit Gorilla right in the middle of his entire mouth. Gorilla didn't even blink. Folks who were there said that Gorilla then hit Basil so hard that his shirttail ran up his back like a window shade. I don't know about that, but I can attest to the fact that for three days, Basil thought he was a bottle of Diet Pepsi.

Well, when Basil came to, he was furious. He told me that he was going to get on Gorilla like white on grits. That very day, he started lifting weights, and in no time at all he had gained ten pounds and made the veins in his arms stick out. When he was convinced he was strong enough, he enrolled in one of those karate schools, and he didn't stop till they had given him one of those black belts that they use to hold up those funny-looking, Japanese pajamas.

Finally, the wiry little sucker said he was ready, and he went looking for Gorilla. Basil found him in the three hundred block of Maple Street. He walked right up, looking straight at the chest, and said, "Gorilla, I'm going to break you up some, 'cause I don't like you and I heard that your mama runs rabbits."

Gorilla broke both of Basil's little wiry legs and knocked out his twelve-year molars. And that proves what I've always said: "The bigger they are, the harder they hit."

Ancestors

It has always been somewhat of a mystery to me how some folks can get caught up in who their ancestors were.

There used to be a lady in our hometown named Miss Emma Henry. When she would introduce herself to someone, she would say, "My name is Emma Henry, and I am a direct descendant of Patrick Henry."

Miss Emma was a bachelor girl till she was about forty; then she married Jeff Hale, who was a short-order cook at the diner. After that, she would always introduce herself by saying, "My name is Emma Henry Hale. I am a direct descendant of Patrick Henry, and my husband is a direct descendant of that great American, Nathan Hale."

Well, for many years, folks around town didn't say much about Miss Emma and her highfalutin ancestors, but one day somebody got tired of her bragging and decided to do some checking.

They started at the courthouse and were able to determine that the most famous relative Miss Emma ever had was a foreman on the third shift at the cotton mill.

It turned out that Hale wasn't really her husband's name. He was using an alias. His real name was Whitlock, and he was wanted in Little Rock, Arkansas, for robbing a Seven-Eleven store.

I will never forget what my granddaddy said when all this came out. He said folks who ain't got nothing to brag about except their ancestors are just like potatoes — the best part of 'em is buried.

Buffy's Tattoo Garden

Just about the time I think I've heard it all, I hear something that's so outrageous it'll absolutely knock a corner post loose.

Have you heard about the national chain of tattoo parlors that's opening? It's called Buffy's Tattoo Garden, and the local franchise owner is a man who calls himself Jasmine. Even before I met him, I knew by his name that he was not from around here.

I thought he might make a pretty good interview, though, so I called old Jasmine. He was very enthusiastic and wanted to tell me about his new fall catalogue of tattoos. He said they have this dandy tattoo for sissy patriots. It's a pink flamingo under a flag. Above the flag it says in big letters, "DISHONOR BEFORE DEATH, OR EVEN DISCOMFORT." He also has a tattoo that says, "BORN TO WALK FUNNY."

He said his big seller is a little tattoo that is a poem inside a heart. It says, "I LOVE SAM, I LOVE SUE; IF YOU'VE GOT A MINUTE, I'LL LOVE YOU, TOO."

I didn't get to know Jasmine all that well during our short interview, but I did have the distinct feeling that he wouldn't last but about twenty minutes at a VFW rally.

Baptism Under Fire

Winslow Hicks was my boyhood friend. Actually, he was more than a friend; he was an important part of my life. You see, Winslow was the first crazy person I ever knew. He was always strange, but when he was about eighteen, he woke up one morning and announced to the world that, during the night, he'd had a vision and was going to start his own religion.

His mama tried to tell him it wasn't a vision, that it was just the beans and franks he ate before going to bed. But Winslow was convinced that he had to start his own religion.

The first thing he did was rent a mobile home and take everything out of it. I mean, he stripped it to the walls. Then he borrowed some folding chairs from the funeral home and put a big sign outside that said "Winslow's Double-Wide Church."

Everybody in town was curious about Winslow's vision, 'cause in my hometown, not many folks had visions. When the sun came up on Sunday morning, everybody for miles around showed up for Winslow's first sermon. His mama even came and sat in the very first row.

Winslow started the sermon by saying that in his vision, a voice had come to him and told him that the key to eternal salvation was for everybody to drive a Henry J automobile, drink RC Colas, and listen to a Motorola radio. He said that was all you had to do to get into heaven.

Well, bless Pat, he barely had the words out of his mouth, when his mama walked up and hit him over the head with one of them folding chairs from the funeral home.

I don't know if it's true or not, but the story is that that was the last time Winslow's mama ever served him beans and franks. I'll tell you one thing: I bet that was the first time in history anybody ever got baptized with a folding chair.

Country Titles

I've told you before about my old friend Lardo DuPree. You'll recall that Lardo is in the business of writing country and western song titles. That's right, he writes only the titles. He figures any fool with a lick of talent can write a country and western song if they've got the right title.

He called me the other day and asked me to come by and look at his new catalogue of titles, and I've got to tell you, I was impressed. In the love department, he had such titles as, "I Like You Better Since You Got a Tattoo," and "She Dropped Dead When I Called Her Fred."

Of course, Lardo doesn't write only love titles; he also writes truck titles, such as the very tender, moving, "Double Clutch Waltz," and "My Radiator's Boiling, But I Don't Need Water."

Some of my favorites are his patriotic titles, like, "Khadafy Needs Cuttin', but We Need His Oil," and "Stomp a Commie in Your Florsheim Shoes."

Actually, I don't think Lardo would mind if I showed you the rest of his new titles, so read 'em and weep:

If You Stomp My Mama One More Time, I'm Gonna Tell on You
You Broke My Heart With Your Nine-Iron Boogie
The Horse You Rode in On
The McCullough Lightweight Blues
Won't You Come Home, Jimmy Hoffa?
Jane Fonda, You Need a Shave
Your Perfume Makes Me Gag, Ruthie
So's Yo' Mama
If My Mule Looked Like You, I'd Leave Him in the Barn
I'd Marry My Truck, but It Ain't Legal
I'd Rather Die Than Have a Vapor Lock
Serving Canned Biscuits Can Get You Cut

He Pawned My Ring and Bought a Goat
You Borrowed My Lawn Mower and My Wife on Alternate Saturdays
My First Husband Was a Polish Joke
Lookin' at You Makes Me Slobber
He Was a Defrocked Priest, but He Sure Could Yodel
Fred Is a Four-Letter Word for Ugly
I'd Rather Sleep With the Hogs than With You When You're Mad
I'd Marry Your Dog Just to Get in the Family
I Love You So Much My Earlobes Hurt
The Holiday Inn Was Made for Us
You Can't Buy Budweiser in Russia
Mama Cussed Castro Till the Day She Died
There'll Be No Commies in Heaven
Burn Rubber, Baby, 'Cause My Name Is Al
Too Much Beer Makes My Mama Sweat
If Caruso Could Have Yodeled, He'd a Been One of Us
My Heart Is Criss-crossed by the Tire Tracks of Your Love
Why Don't You Take My Everlastin' Love and Cram It up Your Heart
Castro Wouldn't Make It at the Heard County Fair
I Love You Better Than My Hog, but He Ain't Never Left Me

Yes sir, that Lardo is a talented fella.

Self-Defense

I've always been interested in self-defense, and after a year of classes and hard work, at long last I have received my black belt. It sure feels good to know that I can protect myself at all times in any situation.

You see, I am a graduate of Shorty's School of Tire Tool, and I am now one of the few people in the world who holds a black belt in tire tool.

I know what you're thinking. You're wondering if tire tool is like karate. No, it's not. Tire tool is an ancient art of self-defense first used by Shorty Jackson, outside the Heard County VFW in 1948. Shorty was attacked that night by three rednecks from Ritter County, and they all knew karate. But Shorty had a tire tool. He put two of them in the hospital and, to this day, the third one is in the Veterans Administration Hospital in Atlanta, sitting in a rocking chair, thinking he is John Cameron Swayze. He just sits there rocking, saying over and over, "It's still ticking. It's still ticking."

From that humble beginning came Shorty's School of Tire Tool. I think their slogan says it all: "Don't be shiftless, don't be lazy; kiss him with a tire tool, he'll think he's John Cameron Swayze."

Willard's Wonder Wieners

My boyhood friend Willard Ledbetter called me one day recently and told me he was about to become rich and famous by opening up a hot-dog joint to end all hot-dog joints. He was going to call it Willard's Wonder Wieners, and he was sure it couldn't miss. His big gimmick, he said, was that he would deliver to your home.

I said, "That's no good; a lot of people deliver."

He said, "In a helicopter? And not just any helicopter, but a helicopter shaped like a giant hot dog, with a big sign across the side that say, 'Willard's Wonder Wieners — We Deliver Within Three Hundred Miles.'"

The highlight of his plan was that the hot dogs were made out of ground chateaubriand, and he was having special buns shipped in daily from a little bakery just outside Paris. I said, "Willard, how much are your Wonder Wieners gonna cost?" He said, "That may be the best part; they're going to be only seven hundred and fifty dollars each." I said, "Willard, nobody in their right mind is going to pay seven hundred and fifty dollars for a hot dog." He answered, "That's why you'll never be a success, Ludlow — you're negative."

Well, I don't know if Willard's business ever got off the ground or not, but just one time, wouldn't you like to taste an all-the-way Willard Wonder Wiener?

Granny's Curses

Granny Porch has just come out with a new list of ancient Irish curses that I want to pass along to you. You see, in 1936, Granny decided that she had used up all of the original ancient Irish curses, so she started to write her own. Let me tell you, they are awesome. Here are some examples of Granny's newest Irish curses:

May Telly Savales not laugh at your joke about a bald-headed Greek.

May your only daughter announce that she is in love with a Los Angeles ram. Not a football player, a Los Angeles ram.

May your Charmin squeeze back.

May your dentist have a fungus on his hands.

May you be forced to listen country/western music until your Ferlin gets Husky.

May your luscious wife win a Gabby Hayes look-alike contest.

May your next child be born wearing water skis.

Now, personally, I don't put much stock in ancient Irish curses. But I would never, ever cross Granny Porch about anything. There are just some things that you can't be too careful about.

Black Cord Fever

Rufus was a victim of the dreaded Black Cord Fever. For you folks out there with no medical background, I guess I should explain.

In the South, when someone gets drunk enough to want to call everybody he ever knew long-distance, he is said to have Black Cord Fever. Rufus had the worst case I ever saw. I used to talk to his loving wife about it.

She was a good, tolerant woman and said, "All he does is have a few drinks and call old Army buddies all over the country on the telephone." I said, "Your phone bill must be enormous." She said, "Well, it could be worse. At least when he gets drunk and gets on the phone, he's at home, not running up and down the highway. I always know where he is, and we always manage someway to pay the phone bill."

Then one day, something very tragic happened. Rufus' wife was checking the phone bill and found a call to San Diego to Shirley's House of Extacy. It seems Rufus had talked to a young lady for thirty minutes; she was known only as "the Whizzer." Well, after his wife found that out, she hit Rufus in the head three times with a very heavy Motorola clock radio. Poor Rufus was dead before he hit the linoleum.

Later, at the funeral, someone asked me how he died. I said Rufus had the world's only terminal case of Black Cord Fever.

A Funny Man

Some people *think* funny, and if you're ever able to find a person who does so, you should spend as much time with them as possible.

I was in the Marine Corps with a guy who was really a funny thinker. His name was Quinton Jerome Murphy, but we all called him Murph.

I remember one night in the barracks, when everybody was sitting around writing letters, shining shoes, and the like. One guy was playing with a can of lighter fluid and a match. Well, the lighter fluid blew up and set this guy's clothes on fire. He panicked and started to run all over the barracks, clothes blazing and screaming his lungs out. I suddenly noticed Murph was screaming, too. He was yelling, "Turn out the lights! Turn out the lights!" Say what you want to about old Murph, but he was a funny, funny man.

One day on the rifle range, the rifle coach was chewing Murphy out. He was jumping up and down, screaming and cussing at old Murph. He said, "Murphy, I've been in the Marine Corps twenty-two years, and you are, without a doubt, the worst shot I have ever seen. You couldn't hit the ground with your hat. You've been firing that M-1 for twenty minutes and ain't hit the target yet. Murphy, you're hopeless." Old Murph looked up and smiled, and said, "Sarge, you really think I can't shoot? See that lieutenant over there? Try to wake him up." That Murphy was a funny, funny man.

In 1954, Murphy got out of the Marine Corps and went back home. He kicked around doing odd jobs. He was a circus P.R. man for a while, but he lost that job when he sold a python to a local stripper to use in her act. Murphy was a funny, funny man.

The last thing I heard from old Murph, he had been elected to Congress. He had just introduced a bill requiring that the national budget be balanced at once, and if it wasn't, the congressmen would be impeached.

Yes sir, old Murph is a funny, funny man.

Floyd's News Conference

One of the things I enjoy most about politics is news conferences. Many times the questions are not asked to get information as much as they are to find out something sensational . . . and sometimes they do.

You can learn a lot about a man from the way he answers questions at a news conference. President Kennedy was my favorite. His news conferences were always laced with that good Irish wit, and no matter how tough the questions got, he generally would have reporters rolling in the aisle at least once.

We had a politician down home who was sort of that way. He could turn the toughest questions around and make a joke. His name was Floyd Jones, and he was the county commissioner for Ritter County. (The county seat is Tex.) I'll never forget his last news conference.

The reporter stood up and said, "Mr. Commissioner, the District Attorney says that you took a ten thousand dollar bribe from an Arab sheik, who wanted to buy the drugstore on the square and raise goats in it. How do you answer that charge?"

The commissioner said, "I deny it, but do you know why the chicken crossed the road? Well, she crossed the road so she could lay it on the line."

"But the D.A.," the reporter interrupted, "has a videotape of you taking the money."

The commissioner smiled and said, "It wasn't me; that was my twin brother. But did you hear the one about the traveling salesman meeting Kate Smith and Roy Acuff at the VFW?"

The reporter interrupted again. "Mr. Commissioner, you don't seem worried about the charges against you."

Ole Floyd smiled and said, "Why should I worry? I've got a plane ticket to Peru and ten thousand dollars in cash in my pocket."

Yes sir, it's men like ole Floyd who make politics more fun than slow-dancing with Dolly Parton.

Aging Gracefully

Advancing age is a reality we all have to face. The very young feel deep down that they are immortal, that they not only will never die, but that they will never age.

But as Father Time starts to lay his gnarled old hand on our shoulders, the realization comes to most of us that there is no fountain of youth, and that in the final analysis, the calendar will have its way.

With this realization, the average fellow will start slowly to accept his gray hair and bifocals, and do his best to grow old with some grace and dignity. There are, however, exceptions to every rule, and some people absolutely refuse to admit that the days grow shorter when you reach September. They seem to fight aging like they have a chance to win. Such a man is Pawpaw Porch.

He absolutely refuses to admit that he is eighty-four years old. How many eighty-four-year-old men do you know who ride a Honda, have a tattoo that says "Born To Raise Hell," and spend all of their spare time chasing cheerleaders? This old man owns the only pair of orthopedic Levis in the country.

I have tried and tried to talk to him about his womanizing, but it does no good. He says to me, "Why don't you mind your own business, you twit? I'm eighty-four years old, and I don't have much time left. I've reached the age where I'm afraid to buy a six-pack, and, besides, cheerleaders are my life. I love their little pom-poms; all I wanna do is touch 'em. It won't hurt them, and it will do me a lot of good." I really think he's hopeless.

I saw something in the want ads yesterday that really worried me. It said "Cheerleaders wanted, no experience necessary. Good working conditions and free Honda rides. For more information, call 555-9966. If a mean-talking old woman answers the phone, hang up."

You know, someday Granny Porch is gonna beat that old man to death.

A Sure Bet

Did I ever tell you about my friend the oddsmaker? I mean, he made Jimmy the Greek seem like a piker. He was known in gambling circles as Leon the Lutheran, but I am here to tell you, when it came to gambling, nothing was sacred. He would bet on how many bodies would be at the local funeral home on Christmas Day. I know that's weird, but the point I'm trying to make is that Leon the Lutheran would bet on anything.

I will never forget the time he won five hundred dollars by betting Milo Pendergrass that he could throw a midget thirty feet. He did it, too. He threw the little sucker out of a fourth-floor window. Yes sir, when it came to winning a bet, Leon would stop at nothing.

I remember the time he bet Walter Ligget a thousand dollars that Walter would be baldheaded within ninety days. Now, Walter had a good, full head of hair, so he took the bet.

Well, bless Pat, it wasn't but about three days later that Walter caught Leon the Lutheran putting Drain-O in his Vitalis. He looked Leon right in the eye and said, "Leon, I'll bet you five hundred dollars you're going to have a concussion within the next fifteen seconds." Leon didn't take the bet, 'cause he saw the tire tool in Walter's hand. You see, even Leon wouldn't bet against a sure thing.

Salesman Supreme

When Benny graduated from high school, he was voted the Boy Most Likely To Succeed. He had a very pleasant personality, and was considered a super salesman even then. One summer, he sold so much White Cloverine brand salve that he won a bicycle and a picture of President Roosevelt, suitable for framing. This may not sound like a big deal, unless you've ever tried to sell salve door-to-door.

When Benny went off to college, everyone knew he would come back a doctor, or a lawyer, or maybe even a CPA. About a month into the first semester, however, Benny's daddy got a call from the dean of men. He said to come get Benny, 'cause he had been expelled and they wanted him off the campus that day.

The story goes that Benny had suffered a Pabst Blue Ribbon attack and, while under the influence, staged a one-man panty raid. Unfortunately, the panty raid had not occurred on campus, but in a local shopping center at 1:30 in the afternoon.

When the police got there, Benny had eleven pairs of ladies' underwear, half of a bra, and a proposal of marriage from a sixty-year-old widow lady. But that's not what had upset the powers at the college; what had riled them was the fact that the coeds on campus were demanding that a dormitory be named in Benny's honor, and they were staging a sit-in in the dean's office that was being led by a sixty-year-old widow lady wearing half a bra.

Benny's daddy brought him home and, about a week later, had him enrolled in a college in New Hampshire. Another month went by and another call came from the college. Seems Benny had suffered another Pabst Blue Ribbon attack, and this time he painted a huge sign on the side of the student union building that said, in six-foot-high letters, "John Wilkes Booth was innocent; Lincoln drew first."

Benny's daddy tried about ten more colleges with the same results.

The last thing I heard about ole Benny was that he had married a sixty-year-old widow lady, and was selling White Cloverine brand salve door-to-door to support them. I don't know how much money he's making, but I'll bet you he's got a bunch of pictures of President Roosevelt.

Reincarnation

I don't believe in reincarnation. Never have and never will. I'm not sure why I'm so closed-minded about it; I guess it's my strict Presbyterian upbringing.

But sometimes I envy folks who do believe in reincarnation. I mean, they can just sit around and think about coming back as somebody rich and famous, or as some kind of exotic animal — like a tomcat. Have you ever thought how nice it would be to come back as a big ole ugly tomcat? Tomcats sleep all day, prowl all night, and never do a lick of work. That's living.

If I did believe in reincarnation, I'd like to come back as Mr. Ellis' '36 Chevrolet. That darling old car lived a life of quiet seclusion that would have made a monk look like Minnesota Fats.

Mr. Ellis worked five and a half days a week. He was a jeweler who got Sunday and half of Wednesday off.

His '36 Chevrolet stayed in the garage at his home all of the time. On Wednesday afternoon, Mr. Ellis would back that old car out of the garage and wash it from top to bottom. Then he would polish it all over, like it was a diamond. Then he would drive it back into the garage and wouldn't take it out again until Sunday, when he would drive his family to Sunday school and church. After church, they would go for a short ride and then put the car up again until it was time to clean it the following Wednesday.

No sir, there's no way I can believe in reincarnation, but for you folks who do, you ought to consider coming back as Mr. Ellis' Chevrolet. You could do a lot worse.

I Cannot Tell a Lie

While doing a little research in American history, I discovered several very interesting facts that are somewhat surprising.

We have heard for many years about the great deeds of our forefathers, but my research shows that without a shadow of a doubt, the real folks we need to thank are our foremamas. For example, we hear a lot about the fact that George Washington never told a lie; well, I have discovered that his mama was responsible for that.

When George Washington was twelve years old, his mama caught him in a lie. History tells us that she picked him up by the front of his little ruffled shirt till his feet were off the floor and she was eye to eye with little George. She said, "Listen to me, wooden tooth. I've about had it with your lying to me. I want you to realize one thing: I brought you into this world, and I can take you out. If you ever tell me another lie, I'm gonna wad up your nose and stick it in your ear." History tells us that George Washington never told another lie.

Then there's the interesting case of Paul Revere. The night that word came down that the British were coming, Paul was laid up in his bed asleep. His mama went in and tried to wake him up. He said, "Not now, mom, I'll get a job tomorrow." Mama Revere said, "Get out of that bed now, you bum. You ain't hit a lick at a snake in six months, and now this big government job just falls in your lap, and all you've got to do is ride that dumb horse and holler. Hit the cobblestones, you loafer, or I'll knock your nose in your watch pocket."

So the next Fourth of July, let's not forget the mothers of this country. Lord knows, there are plenty of them.

Rotunda Johnson

Did I ever tell you about my high school friend, who was probably the strongest teen-aged girl in the history of mankind? Her name was Rotunda Johnson, and she was a great big ole girl. She stood about five-ten and weighed in at almost two-thirty-five.

I'll never forget the time she decided to try out for the football team. She told the coach, whose name was Cleats Wilson, that she wanted to go out for the team, but he told her she couldn't 'cause she was a girl. Rotunda said, "You don't know that for sure, but it shouldn't make any difference, 'cause I'm as big and strong as anybody on the team. Plus, I'm meaner than a snake with a backache."

Well, the coach finally gave her a tryout, but he soon had to drop her from the team, 'cause during the first practice, she put three players out for the season and tore up a blocking sled.

She then went out for the track team, but she had to quit 'cause she kept losing the discus.

She finally found her niche when she made the weight-lifting team. She made the team by bench-pressing the transmission out of a 1937 Hudson Terroplane.

She went on to the Olympics and fell in love with a Cuban weight lifter. They were gonna get married, but the Cuban government wouldn't let him leave the country. The last time I heard, Rotunda was in Key West, Florida, and was planning on swimming to Cuba and bringing her boyfriend out by force. She was already in the water and had a two-by-four with her.

Look out, Mr. Castro; Rotunda Johnson is on her way.

Real Class

"Class" is a difficult word to define, but you always seem to know it when you see it. One of the classiest guys I ever knew was my old boyhood friend Raymond Estees. Now, Raymond had class.

I'll never forget the time he beat up the manager of the theater in our town 'cause the manager had misspelled Johnny Mack Brown's name on the marquee. That was a definite act of class on Raymond's part.

Then there was the time he quit school 'cause the teacher told him the South lost the Civil War. He not only quit school, but he set fire to the teacher's car on the way home.

When Raymond was about eighteen, he joined the Army. When he got to Basic Training, they asked him what job he wanted to be assigned to. He said he didn't care as long as he could kill a lot of Germans. They explained to him that wouldn't be possible, since the second World War had been over for several years. He said, "Well, if I can't kill Germans, who can I kill?" They tried to explain to him that he couldn't kill anybody, because there was no war going on. He said, "O.K., then, if there's no war, you don't need me in the Army." So he came home.

Now, I ask you, is that class? Yes sir, everything that he did was classy. Right now, for instance, ole Raymond is a trustee at Leavenworth Prison. A classy guy, all the way.

Sexaholics Anonymous

I guess everyone on earth has heard about Alcoholics Anonymous, that fine group that does great work. And I think most folks have heard about Gamblers Anonymous, another organization that is helping countless thousands of men and women break the habit of compulsive gambling.

But I have just discovered a group that I'd never heard of before; it's called Sexaholics Anonymous. This is a club that caters to men and women who find they are compulsive adulterers. According to the information in a news release, they say the only requirement for membership is a sincere desire to stop lusting and to help others toward sobriety. This group is based in Simi Valley, California.

I thought this group would make an interesting interview, so I called them long-distance. A lady with a very pleasant voice answered the phone and said, "Sexaholics Anonymous; Mrs. Prone speaking." Well, I told her who I was, and she agreed to give me an interview about the organization.

I said, "How long have you been a member of Sexaholic Anonymous?" Mrs. Prone said, "My, I love your Southern accent." I said, "Thank you, ma'am; now, can you tell me how long you have been associated with Sexaholics Anonymous?" She said, "Nothing on earth turns me on like a man with a Southern accent." I said, "You're very kind; now, would you mind answering me a few questions?" She said, "If I catch an airplane and fly to Atlanta, will you go to bed with me?" I said, "Mrs. Prone, I'm shocked! I'm a married man!" She said, "I'm a married woman, but I'm just not a fanatic about it." Well, we talked for three or four more minutes, but I never did get her to answer any questions.

You know, I don't know for sure how many employees this group has, but I get the distinct impression that they don't get a whole lot of work done.

The Conversation

Every now and then, you see a science fiction movie showing people on other planets who communicate by mental telepathy. I'm sure glad we don't do that here. Think how dull this old life would be if it weren't for good old-fashioned conversation.

Not only do I find it the best form of recreation I know, but you can learn more from talking to folks than you can in school. Longfellow said it best: "A single conversation across the table with a wise man is better than ten years study of books."

History tells us that one of the greatest conversationalists of all time was the Greek philosopher Socrates, and his famous pupil Plato was no slouch in that department, either.

I heard the other day that some new transcripts of conversation between Socrates and Plato had been discovered in a fruit jar that was buried someplace between Bremen and Villa Rica. A copy has been released to the media, and it sure makes fascinating reading.

It starts off when they meet in a saloon, which was called in those days a honky-tonk. I guess they called them honky-tonks 'cause nobody went there but honkys. Anyway, Plato walks up to Socrates' table and says, "Hey, Soc baby, what's happening?" Socrates says, "Those who want fewest things are nearest to the gods." Plato says, "Do what?" Socrates answers, "There is only one good, namely knowledge, and only one evil, namely ignorance." Plato says, "Look, Socrates, you're off work now, so knock off the wise sayings. These folks are gonna think you're a brick short of a load with your dopey talking." Socrates says, "I know nothing except the fact of my ignorance." Plato stands up and says, "Look, Soc, I've had it; it's time you knew the truth. Nobody likes you since you started walking 'round all day trying to talk like Howard Cosell, so I'm gonna give you some good advice: If you don't stop drinking that warm muscatel, you're gonna lose all your friends, 'cause we all think that your brain's gone slick." Socrates says, "Whichever you do, you will repent it."

About that time, Plato hit him in the head with a Miller High Life bottle and left the honky-tonk. That's where the transcript ended.

You know, history sure can be interesting, when you look at it up close.

The Château Switchblade

I never thought I'd live to see the day that I would get all misty-eyed about the demolition of a building. I mean, how can you get emotionally involved with a building?

But let me tell you something, funseekers: I was riding down the highway the other day and discovered, to my horror, that the finest beer joint in the free world was being torn down. Yes sir, the Château Switchblade is gone.

Precious memories, how they linger. I remember the time Monk Moody bench-pressed the juke box.

I remember the time Willie Granger rode his Harley-Davidson into the ladies' bathroom, and the old girls in there were so drunk they didn't notice.

I remember the time Hester Kemp spray-painted the bartender.

I'll never forget the time Jack Wingate got all liquored up and auctioned off his youngest son, Morris.

I remember the time Snake Burnett killed a traveling salesman, when he found out the salesman was from Scranton, Pennsylvania.

I remember the night they held the Wyatt Earp fast-draw contest, and Junior Jackson shot a hole through an "I Like Ike" button. Unfortunately, Herman Johnson was wearing the button at the time.

I remember the neon sign out front that said, "No Food, Just Good Beer."

Yes sir, they have torn down more than a beer joint; they have torn down a legend. I agree with what Jake Cuchaan said. He said tearing down the Château Switchblade is the worst thing to happen since their mule kicked his mama in the belly.

Exchanging Vows – And Blows

I recently attended a friend's wedding, and sitting there in the church, I started remembering some of the weddings I had been to in the past.

Most of them were traditional, with the bride in her long, flowing, wedding dress, and the nervous groom in his tuxedo. The mother of the groom would be crying, 'cause she was losing her baby, and the father of the bride would be crying, 'cause the wedding was costing him about thirty-five hundred dollars.

But not all folks like traditional weddings. You've heard of the baseball fan and his bride who take their vows at home plate during the seventh-inning stretch, or the waitress who gets married in the restaurant so that all of her friends and co-workers can be there. But I guess the most non-traditional wedding I ever attended was when Snake Burnett was going to marry Ruby Lattamore.

It was somewhat of a mismatch from the start, 'cause Snake and Ruby had only one thing in common — they both liked a good fist fight. As a matter of fact, that's how they met; they were both hiding under the same table the night Monk Moody threw a lighted stick of dynamite through the window of the Johnny B. Good Pool Hall.

The plan for the wedding was simple: Snake and Ruby were not only going to exchange vows, they also were going to exchange punches while the preacher performed the ceremony. I guess I should mention at this point that, in addition to being bad to fight, Snake was a little stupid.

It was the night before the wedding, and everybody arrived for the rehearsal. They were in the church parking lot, when Snake started making fun of Ruby's daddy 'cause he drove a Henry J automobile. Well, Snake just kept on and on till he finally made Ruby mad, and she hit him in the head with a tire tool. He didn't die right away; he lived about ten seconds.

Well, the marriage probably wouldn't have worked out anyway, 'cause he was a Methodist, and she was a Presbyterian.

Discipline in School

Whatever happened to discipline in our schools? Not a week goes by that we don't hear or read about the breakdown of discipline in the classroom. People say the children have changed. Poppycock! Children don't change; it's the teachers who have changed. I am amazed when I hear teachers say, "I can't do a thing with these children."

I have always thought that authority, the kind teachers need, was never delegated — it was assumed. The perfect example of this was Lewis, Sr. He *looked* like a teacher. He *thought* like a teacher. He *carried* himself like a teacher. In short, Lewis, Sr., *was* a teacher, and his presence exuded authority.

Once we went to Milledgeville on business, and when the business was finished, we decided to go to a high school basketball game. Neither one of us had been to Milledgeville before, and we didn't know anybody on either team, but we thought that a high school basketball game might be fun.

We were barely settled in our seats when two teen-aged boys came up the aisle beside us. Lewis, Sr., noticed, to his horror, that the boys were not wearing socks. You could see the disgust in his eyes.

In his most authoritative voice, he said, "Boys! Boys! You are not wearing stockings. Who is your homeroom teacher?"

They told him their teacher's name. Lewis, Sr., said, "You are to go directly home and put on stockings. Tell them at the door that you have my permission to leave. And when you have stockings on, you may come back. But boys, if I ever see you at a school function again without stockings, I will personally deliver you to your homeroom teacher. Now go, go, go, go!" And off they went, without a word.

Yes sir, Lewis, Sr., may have had some problems with students, but discipline wasn't one of them. There was never any question about who was in charge.

No, children haven't changed. Teachers have.

My Bird Dog

Did I ever tell you about the worst dog I ever owned? Now, I love dogs and have owned them all of my life, but it was a dark day, indeed, when I was talked into buying Randal. That's right, I owned a dog named Randal.

Randal was a South African Sissy Hound, and when I bought him, the man at the pet store assured me he would be a good watchdog.

I don't know if you've ever seen a purebred South African Sissy Hound, but when they are full grown, they weigh about a hundred and seventy-five pounds and are just great, big old dogs. I was just tickled to death to know that my dog, Randal, was going to keep my home safe from prowlers.

The first time I knew I was in trouble was when I heard Randal bark. He made a strange sound; it came out sort of like, *bowsie wowsie*. Then I really started to worry, because the first time Randal saw a cat, he fainted dead away.

He was, however, very brave when it came to birds. He would stand in the back yard and bark at birds flying over. He would growl and show his teeth and generally go crazy.

I always said old Randal wasn't much of a watchdog, but if a burglar ever came to my house in the middle of the night and brought a bird with him, he was in deep, deep trouble.

I'm Whacko

By Doc of Birmingham

I throw snowballs at the moon,
I eat my grits with an electric spoon,
I wear long johns in May and June,
I'm whacko . . .

Spike Jones music turns me on,
I use Geritol on my lawn,
I party all night, and dance till dawn,
I'm whacko . . .

I got a dog named Henry and a cat named Sue,
I got a wife named Rover and a kid named Blue;
My car won't run, but my skateboard's new,
I'm whacko . . .

Now, I've raced stock cars, and flown airplanes,
Climbed a few mountains, and ridden freight trains;
I even voted for that fellow from Plains,
I'm whacko . . .

My daughter's fat, and my son is puny,
My wife is kinda "Looney Tooney,"
My mother thinks she's Mickey Rooney,
I'm whacko . . .

Now, some think I'm crazy, but that's not true,
I brush my teeth with Superglue,
I put it in my Kool-aid, too,
I'm whacko . . .

If *you* feel a little strange, and don't know where to go,
I can tell you what to do:
Go sit on the porch with ole Ludlow . . .
Then *you* will be a wacko, too!

Land of Opportunity

There are some things in life that will absolutely drive you crazy— like when you can't think of somebody's name that you know you should know. And things like, who in the world is Rula Lenska?

Now, that shouldn't bother me, but when she comes on TV and smiles and says, "Hi, I'm Rula Lenska," it drives me to distraction. To the best of my knowledge, I've never heard of Rula Lenska; but the way she says her name, you know she expects you to know who she is.

We do know that she uses a lot of hair spray. As a matter of fact, they had a television picture of her one time, standing on a bridge with about a ninety-mile-per-hour wind blowing, and not a hair was out of place.

Well, this thing about who she is got to be so important to me, that one day I just picked up the phone and called her. I thought it was kind of strange that the area code was for Chattanooga, Tennessee, but I called anyway. Rula answered the phone and said, "Double Eagle Café." I told her who I was, and that I wanted to know how she got on television. Well, she told me the dangest story.

It seems that Rula's real name is Shirley Bang, and she owns the Double Eagle Café in Chattanooga. This hair spray company had sent a man by, and they had hired her to play like she was a movie star from London. They paid her the minimum wage and all the hair spray she could squirt on her head.

The story goes that they tried to hire Junior Samples, but he had a hard time with English — not the accent, the language.

Yes sir, where else but in America can a girl like Shirley Bang make all that money 'cause her hair is all plastered down?

The Psychiatrist

I recently ran into an old boyhood chum named Bismark Calhoun. Bismark grew up to become a psychiatrist. Now, that didn't surprise me much, 'cause even as a child, Bismark was kind of strange.

The day we met and renewed our old acquaintance, he invited me to his house for dinner. I've gotta tell you, I never spent a longer evening in my life.

During dinner, he said, "I notice, Ludlow, you are not drinking your water." I said, "That's right, Bismark." He said, "There could be many reasons for your rejection of the water. You could hate your mother, or perhaps you were never able to identify with your siblings. Or," he continued, "you may have certain sexual hang-ups regarding the Mills Brothers and a Sears Die-Hard battery. Or, you may feel your space is being invaded by the water glass." He said, "It's all right, Ludlow, you can tell me. I'm your friend and a licensed psychiatrist. Tell me, why didn't you drink your water? I'll try to understand." I said, "Bismark, I didn't drink my water 'cause there's a dead cockroach in it."

Boy, I'm really glad he's a psychiatrist, 'cause I've known for years that it takes one to know one.

English Is a Foreign Language

Changing Meanings

Have you ever noticed how our language is changing? So many new words and new meanings have crept into the language that, if we're not careful, we'll wake up one morning and won't be able to understand each other. Let me give you a few examples:

When did the color brown start to be known as earth tones, and why don't people say brown anymore?

When did a settee become a sofa, and whatever happened to davenports and chifforobes?

When did personality become charisma, and when did a he-man turn into a macho man?

When did a straight stick become four-in-the-floor, and why and when did James Stewart suddenly become Jimmy Stewart?

When did dope fiends turn into junkies, and then into drug abusers? When did folks who drink too much turn into alcohol abusers? They are certainly not abusing alcohol; they are abusing their bodies. But nobody ever calls them body abusers.

When did dirty pictures become porn, and not-quite-so dirty pictures become soft porn?

When did baseball teams become ominous? In my day, King Kong was ominous.

When did countries start being underdeveloped? Just a few years ago, Charles Atlas could take care of anything underdeveloped. And why are some countries called "emerging nations," and how long before they quit emerging and become just regular ol' nations?

When did a used car become a preowned automobile, and when did a deodorant become an anti-perspirant?

When did fat girls become full-figured, and when did friendship become an interpersonal relationship?

When did a den become a great room, and when did a xylophone become vibes? And when did a split end become a wide receiver?

When did too much of anything become a glut? And when did the War Department become the Defense Department?

Yes sir, if this keeps up, someday you're going to need an interpreter to talk to your milkman.

Stupid Questions

Is it just my imagination, or are people asking more stupid questions than ever before?

For example, I pulled into a gas station the other day, and this ol' slack-jawed boy came walking out and said, "Can I do something for ya?" Now, bear in mind, I had just driven my car into his gas station, taken great care to get my tank close to his gas pump, and he says, "Can I do something for ya?" I said, "Yeah, I got this wisdom tooth that's been bothering me; can you take a look at it?" Now, that's not an extreme example, 'cause these things happen to me all the time.

I was fishing one day from a boat dock, and had caught a string of ten or twelve bream. While I was sitting there, a total stranger walked up, looked at my string of fish, and said, "Did you catch those fish?" I said, "No, actually I talked them into surrendering."

There was also the time my car overheated on the expressway about forty miles from any exit. The car was sitting there with steam coming out of everything; it looked like I was sitting in the middle of a giant London fog.

I was afraid the car was gonna blow up, so I got out of it and was standing there watching these clouds of steam boil out when a policeman pulled up. He said, "Are you having car trouble?" I said, "No, actually I was just about to steam some clams. Would you like to join me?"

You know what? I don't think that's any reason to put a man in jail.

Pebbles and Pops

It seems to me that television has changed the way we talk. Lately I've heard some things said that, years ago, you never would have heard anybody in the South say. Let me give you a few examples:

I heard a child the other day say he had a bag of shiny pebbles. Now, as a child, I knew what a pebble was. It was what people up north called small rocks. I never heard them referred to in the South as pebbles. I guess if I had been asked on a school test what a pebble was, I probably would have answered that it was a little bitty yankee rock.

Same thing applies to soft drinks. I was grown before I knew that a pop or a soda was nothing on earth but a Coca-Cola, or a Pepsi, or a Big Orange. I still don't know why they call 'em pop.

I asked a friend of mine from Pennsylvania, and he said they got that nickname for soft drinks because of the sound they make when you open them. That's the silliest thing I've ever heard of.

Anybody with the brain of a tire iron knows that soft drinks don't go "pop" when you open them; they go "whoosh." Champagne goes "pop." Weasels go "pop." But soft drinks go "whoosh."

Well, I guess things like that work themselves out, 'cause it would sound kind of strange to hear a teen-aged boy invite his girl out for a cold "whoosh."

Gimme a What?

I thought I had heard about everything there was, but I guess we live and learn. Seems that somebody in pro football decided the games would be more exciting if they wrote some new cheers for the cheerleaders. They said that "rah-rah" and "gimme an A" was O.K. for high school and college, but they thought pro cheerleaders were too sophisticated for that.

So the NFL has come up with an entire new list of pro cheers. I thought you might enjoy hearing a few of them.

What do you think about this one? "Don't leave now, their defense we will wreck it. And if you stay till the third quarter, we'll all get naked." Or the one the Forty-Niners will be using soon: "Our team's great, our team's fine. Hey there, big boy, what's your sign?" Or this one from the Dallas cheerleaders: "Our clothes are tight, our modesty is less, but we sure love a man with an American Express."

I think one of my favorites is the Green Bay Packers' new one that goes, "Our Packers are rough, our Packers are tough, but it's kind of disgusting, 'cause they all dip snuff." Or this one, from a team I'd rather not identify: "Our team's just great, it has flavor. But keep an eye on the coach, 'cause he's a white slaver."

No wonder baseball is still the national pastime.

Chortling

Perfectly good words seem to be falling out of our language. I mean, one week a word is used, and the next week it's gone.

I tell you this with a heavy heart, because one of my favorite words has disappeared. It was always one of my favorites, but anytime I used it, people looked at me like I was some kind of a nut. The word is *chortle.* Think about that — a perfectly darling little word. I can't speak for anyone else, but I, for one, am very much into chortle.

When President Carter said, "I will never lie to you," a lot of folks sneered. Not me; I chortled. I chortled so much it made me sweat.

When the FBI caught those gravy-sucking congressmen in Abscam, I dang near made myself sick, chortling. When Richard Nixon said, "I'm not a crook," I fell out of my chair, chortling.

I come from a long line of chortlers. My uncle Enrico Porch was one of the world's first singing chortlers. As a matter of fact, he literally died chortling. You see, his wife asked him one day if he had it to do all over again, would he still marry her. He chortled, and she killed him with a nine iron. Which goes to prove what I've always said: Chortling at the wrong time will get you killed.

Language Barrier

It's a wonder to me that folks new to this country ever learn to speak the language. I mean, it's tough enough on those of us who have been here a long time, so think what a foreigner must have to go through trying to speak American.

For example, have you ever swoggled a horn? Now, think about that for a minute. When you say you have been hornswoggled, just what does that mean?

And what in the name of Lash LaRue is a galoot? And why do we consider people to be a shiftless? Or have you ever in your entire life known anyone who buckled a swash? And why do we call longjohns, longjohns? Why not longfreds, or short-ralphs? And why do we call a floozy a floozy?

Did you ever hear of a bushwhacker who whacked a bush? Or a guy who took the time to dry out a gulch? And while we're on the subject, what is a gulch? What is a pass, and why do they always cut people off there? Why doesn't a cowboy say he'll cut them off at Whiteway and Main streets, or he'll cut them off just the other side of the Dairy Queen?

What do people mean when they say dagnabbit? And have you ever wondered why some people just leave, while others just mosey along? And some folks split, or cut out, or vamoose.

Yes siree, strangers in this country have a tougher time every year with the language. They must, 'cause I do.

Strange Things

Have you ever noticed all the strange things that happen in the world everyday? If you stop and think about it, there's a lot of things going on that I don't think anybody understands.

For example, why is it that you never run out of Tabasco sauce? I can only assume, from that simple fact, that a small bottle of Tabasco sauce will last the average family a lifetime. That's strange.

Why is it that when you go into a gas station, you find that they have locked the bathroom and left the cash register unlocked? That strikes me as strange.

Why do musicians always say, "Take it from the top?" Seems to me, if they took it from the bottom, it would be a very short song.

Why do we call a hot water heater a hot water heater? Actually, it's a cold water heater. Doesn't that strike you as strange?

Why do professional air traffic controllers call themselves that? Does that mean that someplace there are amateur air traffic controllers?

Why do they sell life insurance at airports and not at bus stations? I find that strange.

Yes sir, the longer I live, the more I'm convinced that it's a strange, strange world.

A Brand-New Word

Have you heard the latest word to creep into our language? Are you ready for this? It's *bi-coastal,* and it refers to someone who spends a lot of time on each coast of the United States.

They invented it so that at a cocktail party you can say, "Oh, that's my friend Hazel. She's bi-coastal, you know." Now, I ask you, isn't that the most pretentious thing you've ever heard?

Well, I've decided our language can be greatly improved, if we come up with some more words that are just as pretentious as bi-coastal.

Here's my list, and maybe you can add to it:

Bi-drunk, as in "My friend Leon was bi-drunk last night." That means that Leon got drunk in two different beer joints.

Or how 'bout *bi-ugly,* as in "Eunice Mae is bi-ugly." That means Eunice Mae is twice as ugly as a two-day-old cantaloupe rind.

Or perhaps *bi-short.* That means that someone is so short, they have to stand in a chair to tie their shoe laces.

Or how 'bout *bi-crooked.* That means somebody is twice as crooked as John Dillinger, and in all likelihood is seeking public office.

What's Your Phobia?

I have been doing a little research about phobias, and I have discovered a very interesting fact. Did you know that almost everybody has some kind of phobia?

I started my research after reading a story about a lady in Tennessee who sued Knox County and the city of Knoxville for twenty-five thousand dollars. It seems that a wall-mounted toilet in the city-county building fell to the floor with her on it. The woman claimed, in her suit, that she now suffers from a fear of toilets, and is forced to search for toilets that are securely attached to the floor.

After reading this story, it occurred to me that a lot of folks have phobias that don't have names, and everyone knows that it's no fun having a nameless phobia. So I have set about to name some unnamed phobias.

For example, the lady I just told you about has toilet phobia. My Uncle Fergie has for years been afraid of his wife beating him up while he was asleep; he suffers from what I call nocturnal knuckle phobia. Here are a few more phobias that you need to know about:

Gazoonga phobia: an unnatural fear of bumping into Dolly Parton
Cosell phobia: a fear of long words with no meaning
Phobia aphobia: an unnatural fear of phobias
Formica phobia: a fear of sitting nude on a cold counter top
Claustrophobia: an unnatural fear of claustros
Dab phobia: a fear of Brillcream
Falsetto phobia: a fear of Slim Whitman

You may rest easy, my friends, for my research goes on. As a matter of fact, I am trying to name a phobia now that causes me to break into a cold sweat everytime I hear the word, Cleveland.

The Name Game

Who said, "What's in a name?" Whoever it was, I've forgotten his name. I do remember, however, that it's very important to pick the right name for your child. If you choose the wrong name, the child is going to be limited for the rest of his, or her, life. No matter how much talent, ambition, or drive the child may have, it could be doomed to certain failure because of a badly chosen name.

Let me give you a few examples:

If, by chance, you named your son Rula, he could never be a professional wrestler, a lumberjack, or a bartender.

If you named your son Fred, he could never grow up to own his own Chinese restaurant. I mean, how would a sign look that said, "Fred's Chinese Restaurant?"

If you named your daughter Hester, she could never grow up to be the belle of society. I know that 'cause the Vanderbilts had a bunch of children, and not a one of 'em was named Hester.

If you named your son Bruce, he could never grow up to be a hair stylist. I mean, after all, a guy named Bruce has got enough trouble. Right?

If you named your daughter Roxy, she could never grow up to be a ballerina.

So remember: You have an obligation to pick your child's name carefully. I should know, 'cause I'm Ludlow Porch.

Taking Orders

We get ordered around every day by absolute strangers. I mean, everywhere we go, we see signs that say Push, Pull, Exact Change Only, No Tank Tops, Authorized Personnel Only, Cash Only, No Smoking, Keep Off the Grass, and on and on.

None of these orders bothers me much, but there's one that really does get my nanny goat. It affects every one of us, and it's high time we did something about it. It says, "Follow Label Instructions." Now, that just violates every concept of the American system.

How dare some stranger tell me that I must follow his directions! A person whom I know nothing about. He may not be from a good family, or he could be some kind of a wild, mad scientist, out to destroy nasal drip as we know it. Following this fella's instructions could be disastrous.

The instructions should say something like this: "Dear Customer, you bought this product. You paid for it with your hard-earned money. It is yours; you own it. Therefore, feel free to use it in any way that you like. Put it on your hair, if you want, or you might try rubbing it on your feet. Gargle with it, or put it on your fern. It's your property, dear customer, and we couldn't care less what you do with it."

When the free enterprise system comes out with a product with that kind of label, I'll be the first to buy it, and I won't care one way or the other whether it works or not.

Metric Nonsense

I haven't figured out the metric system yet, but I am sure about it — I'm sure I don't understand it, and I'm pretty sure nobody else does. It's the biggest mess since my cousin Doodle poured Karo syrup over his ant farm. The worst thing about the metric system is that it will kill some of our best clichés.

For example, do you remember how your grandmother always said, "Give him an inch, and he'll take a mile?" You wouldn't have paid her a bit of attention, if she'd said, "Give him 2.5 centimeters and he'll take l. 69 kilometers." That just sounds silly.

And how about that ugly girl in your third-period history class? Nobody would say, "I wouldn't touch her with a three-meter pole."

Telling your girlfriend you love her a bushel and a peck is fine, but to say, "I love you a kilogram and a gram and a hug around the neck," would make you sound like a dang fool.

I'll tell you what I want to see. I want to see the first guy walk into Mr. Juhan's store and tell ole Buford that he wants a liter of buttermilk, 'cause Buford is apt to cut him.

Wise Old Sayings

A lot of wise old sayings won't hold water when you examine them closely.

For example, I'm just tickled to death that life's not a bowl of cherries. Think about the implications of life being a bowl of cherries — it'll absolutely boggle your mind.

And how about this one — You always hurt the one you love. That's dumb, 'cause sometimes you hurt folks you don't give a damn about.

One of my least favorites is, Behind every dark cloud, there's a silver lining. That's just not so; behind a lot of dark clouds there is a tremendous rainstorm.

And anybody with a lick o' sense knows that a stitch in time will not save nine. A stitch in time will save six, tops.

Not only that, but an apple a day will dang near kill you.

And, too many cooks won't spoil the broth, 'cause broth ain't fit to eat in the first place.

Yes sir, if you look at wise old sayings, you will find that a lot of them are just plain dumb.

Those Days of Yore

The Service Station

The other day I was pumping my own gas at one of those chrome and plastic gas stations. You know — the ones where you pay some guy who's sitting in a glass cage, and you don't even know his name, and he doesn't even recognize you, because he's too busy reading the latest magazine to be bothered with customers.

I thought to myself that buying gas shouldn't be such an impersonal transaction; it should be a warm, fun thing to do, like it used to be at Charlie Watson's gas station. Charlie was a good ole boy and sure knew how to run a gas station.

You'd pull up to one of Charlie's two pumps, and he'd come out to the car, wiping his hands on a rag. I don't think Charlie ever came out to my car that he wasn't wiping his hands. He'd smile and say, "Hey, Luddie, can I hep ya?" I'd tell him to give me a dollar's worth of regular. Charlie would say, "If you buy five gallons, you get a free cup and saucer." I'd say, "O.K., Charlie, make it five gallons." And Charlie would say, "If you buy ten gallons, we give you the cup and saucer and throw in three iced tea glasses with a picture of Wonder Woman on each glass."

Then Charlie would pump the gas, clean my windshield, and check my oil. He'd then fill me in on all the town gossip and offer to buy me a soft drink. Before I left, he would offer to check the air in my tires. When I was driving out, he would always yell out to me, "Come see us."

Old Charlie had a heart attack about 1955 and died. He was a good fellow and knew more about selling gas than anybody I ever knew. You know, if it were possible, I'd buy a hundred gallons of gasoline for just one Wonder Woman iced tea glass.

The Old Comics

I was watching television the other night, and there was a young comic doing a stand-up routine. I have to admit that he was kind of funny, but in watching him, I noticed that most of the jokes he was using were either a little off-color or had a sharp point he was sticking in some politician.

It started me thinking about the great comedians of the past, and the sad fact that no one has come along to replace them. I thought about Groucho, Chico, and Harpo, and realized they are gone forever.

It made me sad to realize that Bud Abbot and Lou Costello have done "Who's on first?" for the last time. I wondered what Will Rogers would say about today's state of the union, and what comments W. C. Fields would make about Donnie and Marie.

How would those two wonderful clowns, Laurel and Hardy, handle the producer who wanted them to put four-letter words and off-color clichés into their movies and their routines?

I thought how much I miss the Ritz Brothers, Emmett Kelley, and Jack Benny. I thought about Herb Shriner, Fred Allen, and Jimmy Durante. I thought about Edgar Bergen, and Charlie McCarthy, and Buster Keaton.

I thought about all of the funny men of the past who have gone, and I came to one inescapable conclusion: The angels must have rejoiced when they saw them coming.

Sissies

What has happened to sissies? When I was growing up, every year in school there was at least one sissy in my class. But today I rarely hear the word, and the sissies themselves seem to be gone.

Sissies were easy to spot in those days. For one thing, they always dressed well. You would never find a sissy wearing Levis or blue jeans; they always wore dress pants, well-starched shirts, and dress shoes.

And, sissies always talked proper; you never, ever heard a sissy say ain't, and they used all of the big words they could possibly come up with. Why, they even called their mama mother. Sissies usually made all A's in school, especially in conduct.

Sissies had no idea what Joe DiMaggio's batting average was, and the thing that really used to hack me off was that they didn't even care if the Crackers lost a three-game series to Little Rock. Sissies did not like Durango Kid movies. Sissies took music lessons, and didn't mind when they had to practice. Sissies never got skates for Christmas; they got chemistry sets and argyle socks. Sissies never played ball or rode bicycles; they couldn't because, first and foremost, it was against the sissy code to sweat.

I guess by now you have the impression that, as children, we judged other people pretty harshly. That's one of the nice things about being a grown-up: We never judge people by the way they dress, or how they talk, or the color of their skin, or how much money they make.

But for some strange reason, to this very day, I wouldn't be caught dead in a pair of argyle socks.

That Old Magic

There are a lot of problems with growing up. I mean, being an adult is no picnic. But the biggest problem with growing up is that you stop believing in the magic that is a big part of your life.

Don't you remember the magic and wonder that were all around you as a child? Do you remember when you looked under your pillow in the morning, found a nickel, and knew for the first time the magic of the tooth fairy?

Do you remember after church, brand-new clothes, straw baskets with fake green straw, a laughing grandfather, and discovering all by yourself the magic of the Easter Bunny?

Do you remember the new baby at your house? The excitement and delight, and the magic of the stork bringing that beautiful baby?

I hope that as you have grown up, you have not forgotten all of the magic we knew at one time in our lives, because it's always been there.

If you don't believe me, next Christmas morning, look deep into the eyes of any three-year-old. You'll see it.

Convenience Stores

I never go into one of those modern convenience stores without feeling a little bit of sadness. You see, I know what a store is *supposed* to look like. I know what they are *supposed* to sell, and the new stores don't come close on either count.

First of all, the store must be wooden; a brick store is entirely unacceptable. Next, there must be two gas pumps out front — one marked Regular and the other marked Ethyl. In addition, there should be a kerosene dispenser where you can buy a dime's worth of kerosene, if your whim dictates. Over the kerosene dispenser, there should be a large metal sign that says "Tube Rose Snuff."

To gain entrance into this most wonderful place, you must pass through double screen doors, and on each door is written in bright yellow, "Colonial Is Good Bread."

Once inside, you see a lot of signs on the walls. You see a big metal sign that says, "Red Rock Ginger Ale — 5¢." Another sign says, "I'd Walk a Mile for a Camel," and a small green sign, made out of cardboard, says, "Repent or Burn in Hell."

On a wooden counter that runs the entire length of the store, you will find a hoop of the most delicious, beautiful cheese you have ever seen. Beside the cheese is a punchboard, where you can win a single-shot, .22 rifle for just a nickel; second prize is a color picture of the Last Supper, suitable for framing. There is also a jar of colored jaw-breakers and another full of cookies, and beside that is a display for Prince Albert. The sign says buy two cans of Prince Albert and get a genuine briar pipe free.

And let's not forget my favorite — the drink box. It must be red with the sliding door on the top. It has the remains of a twenty-five-pound block of ice floating around that freezing-cold water.

Now, *that* was a real convenience store.

The Carnival

I love the new amusement parks that you see nowadays, but somehow they don't have the character of the old-time carnivals — the ones that came to town on trucks, found themselves a vacant lot, brought out the Kewpie dolls, turned on the neon, and went to work.

I can smell the onions frying now. I can hear the sideshow barker chanting, "Just one dime, the tenth part of a dollar, to see Jojo, the Dog-Faced Girl. She walks, she talks, she crawls on her belly like a reptile." Boy, how I miss Jojo, the Dog-Faced Girl.

I miss Madam Revolta, the fortune teller, too. I miss the amazing Leon, the man who could swallow his own nose. I miss seeing the car that Bonnie and Clyde were killed in.

I even miss the nasty looking guys who ran the games and always overcharged you, and then tried to short-change you, to boot. I miss the old winos who used to run the Ferris wheel.

I miss the strip shows that I was never quite old enough to get into. You know the ones I mean; where the girls came out on the stage on the midway and got about three-quarters naked. Then the barker told the crowd that for a quarter, they could come inside and see those same ole girls get slap naked.

I've never had any desire to see a world's fair, but I sure would like to go to one of those dinky old carnivals just one more time.

Video Games

My young son Charlie walked up to me the other day and asked, "Can I have a new cartridge for my video game?"

"What's it called?" I countered.

"It's real neat," he said. "It's called 'Blow a Martian's Guts Out.'"

"How much is it?"

"It's on sale for only a hundred and thirty-seven dollars," he said.

"Are you nuts? A hundred and thirty-seven dollars for a video game? You can't have it, and I don't want to hear another word about it."

"Aw, gee whiz," he moaned. "Now I'll never get to blow a Martian's guts out."

I thought at once about the toys I used to get. One Christmas I got a doctor's bag. It had a plastic hypodermic needle, a tongue depressor, a phony stethoscope, and a little bottle of red pills that were cinnamon flavored. They were delicious. Another time I got a vacuum cleaner, and my mother told me I could use it any time I wanted to.

But I'll tell you the best toy that I ever had. It was the box that our new refrigerator came in. It was a combination clubhouse, submarine, and airplane. As a matter of fact, it could be anything you wanted it to be.

I played in it for hours and hours. I made it the first nuclear-powered submarine, way back there in my Buck Rogers days. I also made it a bomber and was one of the first people to fly over and bomb Tokyo, during the war. It was a many-splendored thing.

You can say what you want to about video games, or any other games or toys for that matter. As far as I'm concerned, the best toy maker in the world is still Frigidaire.

WW II Memories

I was a small child during the second World War. Therefore, my memories of that time are special, at least special to me.

I remember that I could no longer take a penny to the store and buy a piece of Double Bubble gum. I remember that Mr. Allen was our neighborhood air raid warden.

I remember the meatless Tuesdays, victory gardens, and the air-raid drills at school.

I remember Bob Hope from the radio, cracking jokes about Hitler, Mussolini, and Tojo, and I remember the pride I felt when I told my playmates that my Uncle Buddy was a Marine.

I remember the sailor hat my Uncle Simpson sent me from the Pacific, and I remember our national heroes, like Eisenhower, Patton, and MacArthur.

I remember my own personal heroes, like my Uncle Tom and Uncle Walt, who were fighting the Germans in a place called Europe.

I remember that the streets downtown were full of people hugging and kissing and dancing. I remember a group of people in the midst of that celebration holding hands at Five Points, and singing "God Bless America."

I remember my grandmother crying that day, because her boys were coming home.

V-J Day was a special day for me and for the world.

Rich Things

Do you remember, when you were a child, what you thought only rich people had? I guess the movies were responsible for our views, but I remember that in my mind, only rich people had things like wall-to-wall carpet or extension telephones.

Only rich folks had purebred dogs or deep freezers. Certainly, only the rich could afford central heat, and only rich people had air conditioning. As a matter of fact, the only air conditioning in my hometown was at the local picture show.

Do you remember when you thought that only rich people had one-party telephone lines, and that only rich people could take a trip on an airplane?

I knew for sure that only rich people could afford to ride in taxis. But that wasn't a big problem in our town, because it was so small we didn't have a taxi company.

It never occurred to us to brood or worry about these missed luxuries, 'cause we had things like lemonade, tire swings, rubber guns, and Captain Marvel comic books. We had fried steak and mashed potatoes; we had yo-yos, and Johnny Mack Brown movies. We had Li'l Abner, all-day singings, and dinner on the grounds.

Yes sir, every night when I say my prayers, I thank the Lord for what I have now and for what I had then.

A Dying Memory

Some of my fondest memories revolve around railroads. I can recall being in bed at night, listening to that long, low whistle in the distance, and wondering where that train was going. What wonderful adventure was it taking its passengers toward?

I can remember during the second World War, when, as a small child, I went to the old Terminal Station to watch trains take my uncles off to fight. I remember the sadness I felt watching the wives and the girlfriends of the soldiers, crying after the trains pulled out of the station. I remember the happiness after the war, when the trains brought the men home again. I can remember straining to look at the soldiers' faces as they got off the train, hoping that I could see a familiar one.

I remember when I was ten years old and got to ride to Florida by myself to visit my aunt and uncle.

I remember the sadness I felt when the train station fell to the old wrecking ball. I wondered why nobody was upset about it except me.

I remember how much fun it was, as an adult, to ride the Southern Crescent to New Orleans to watch Georgia play in the Sugar Bowl.

I remember Pullman cars and redcaps and gray-headed men saying, "All aboard!"

Now they tell us that the trains in many parts of the country probably will be gone before long. It looks to me like the older I get, the more old friends I lose.

So Long, Joe

When the radio announcer said a couple of years ago that former heavyweight champion Joe Louis was dead at the age of sixty-six, I had an almost uncontrollable urge to cry. No, I never met Joe Louis, but when I heard he was gone, I knew that another part of my childhood was gone.

While I was never privileged to know him, or even to see him in person, I learned a lot from the Brown Bomber. For example, I learned that even though you can do something better than anybody else on earth, the character of the man comes in the deed itself, not in bragging about what you did or what you are going to do.

You see, Joe Louis was a quiet, modest champion — something we haven't seen much of in recent years. I guess the only thing to do now is to hang on to our memories that the champ left us.

Memories like the Billy Conn fights. Memories of the famous Louis left jab, that was so quick that it photographed as a blur. Memories of the short right that nobody ever threw with better results than Joe. Memories of Joe Louis telling the newsreel reporters of 1942 that we were going to win the war 'cause God was on our side. Memories of his quiet, soft drawl as he was being interviewed by hundreds of reporters. Memories of Rocky Marciano actually crying after he knocked Louis out. Rocky wasn't crying out of happiness; you see, Joe Louis was his boyhood hero, too.

Joseph Louis Barrow, an Alabama sharecropper's son, who grew up to be champion, soldier, and gentleman — not necessarily in that order. Dead at sixty-six. So long, champ; we may never see your like again.

Good Old Days

It's a wonder to me that any of us survive our teen years. I hope I can remember what difficult years they were the next time I get impatient with my teen-agers.

Admittedly, we had different problems from theirs, but over the long haul, I suspect a teen-age problem is like sin — it doesn't change much over the years.

Do you remember how the tiniest pimple could look as big as a well bucket if you discovered it the night before a big dance? And do you remember how awful your girl's hair looked the day after her mama had given her a Tonette?

Do you remember the pure terror that swept over you when you got out of the shower in the morning and discovered you were out of Stoppet, and you had these thoughts of starting to smell like a goat during third-period English? Do you remember how it felt when you called a girl for a date and she said no, and the only reason she would give was that she had other plans? You found out later that those plans were six-foot-two inches tall and drove a convertible.

Do you remember the sadness you felt losing a football game, or a library book, or the new girl's phone number, or a hubcap?

It always makes me wonder why we call the good old days, the good old days.

Where Are You, Rula Lenska?

I often think about things from my past that I miss — like church bells and minor-league baseball. But it just occurred to me that there are a lot of things from my past that I *don't* miss. As a matter of fact, I'm glad to see 'em gone.

Things like Rula Lenska commercials. I can't even remember what she was selling. All I can remember is that she was a famous actress who nobody ever heard of.

I'm also glad that people don't put homemade mustard plasters on children anymore. My grandmother could make a mustard plaster that smelled so bad it would cause wallpaper to peel in the next county.

I'm glad we don't have telephone party lines anymore.

I'm glad little boys don't wear corduroy knickers anymore. You remember standing by the radiator in school on rainy days, so your corduroy knickers could dry out? Nothing on earth smells as bad as wet, corduroy knickers.

And I'm glad that teen-aged boys don't have Beatle haircuts anymore. Who wants to see a world full of teen-aged boys with no foreheads?

And I'm glad we don't have ice boxes in our homes anymore.

No doubt about it: Nostalgia just ain't what it used to be.

Double Bubble

Have you ever stopped to think of the good things that pass out of your life when you are grown? Some things we outgrow, and some things we get too sophisticated to do. For example, when was the last time you had a piece of Double Bubble gum? Do you remember the taste of Double Bubble? Vastly superior to chateaubriand, if I do say so myself.

And when was the last time you had a good piggyback ride? Do you remember how much fun it was when you could ride piggyback on somebody?

And how about walking barefooted in the mud? I don't remember why I did it, but I do remember it was great fun.

And do you remember how much fun it was to put on your bathing suit and have somebody squirt you with the garden hose? Boy, that first squirt was cold as ice, but once you got soaked, it was great fun.

When was the last time you read a good Captain Marvel comic book, or skipped rocks across the lake, or rode a bicycle with no hands?

When was the last time you showed off in front of a girl, or got a brand-new pocket knife for your birthday? When was the last time you played with a frog, swung on a rope, or went to a wiener roast? When was the last time you went to a prom party, or went skinny-dipping?

When was the last time you read *Treasure Island*, or saw a Durango Kid movie?

You know what I think? I think being a grown-up isn't all it's cracked up to be.

Take It from
Ludlow . . .

Bad Days

There's no need to speculate about whether or not you're going to have a bad day. I say this because I have determined over the years several sure-fire ways to tell if you're in for a rough one. These will never let you down:

You know you're going to have a bad day when you call home and a fireman answers the phone.

You know you're going to have a bad day when you discover that your teen-aged daughter has a Holiday Inn credit card.

You know you're going to have a bad day when the IRS sets up a field office in your carport.

You know you're going to have a bad day when your twin brother forgets your birthday.

You know you're going to have a bad day when the suicide prevention bureau hangs up on you.

You know you're going to have a bad day when the manufacturer recalls your pacemaker.

You know you're going to have a bad day when you discover that your teen-aged son is dating a girl who has a disease named after her.

You know you're going to have a bad day when your teen-aged daughter comes home at six A.M. carrying a Gideon Bible.

You know you're going to have a bad day when you find out that your three-year-old has just fed a box of Ex-Lax to your Saint Bernard.

You know you're going to have a bad day when you discover termites have just eaten your sofa.

You know you're going to have a bad day when your daughter tells you she just won a scholarship to Guido's School of Massage.

You know it's going to be bad when you discover your commode is stopped up and your cat is missing.

And you really know it's going to be a bad day when your local undertaker sends you an estimate.

You don't have to wonder whether or not it's going to be a bad day; Mother Nature will let you know.

Non-Status Seekers

The world is full of status seekers — folks who must drive a certain model car and live in a certain neighborhood. You'll always find them at the country club carrying an attaché case (with a peanut butter and jelly sandwich inside) and a three-months-old copy of the *Wall Street Journal*. To these people, status is everything.

But there is another group of people I want to address. These are the non-status seekers, and they have their symbols, too. I have decided to make a list of the non-status symbols, so that you can decide which category you fall into. Here are some non-status symbols:

1. Pink flamingos in the front yard
2. A wide tie with gravy stains
3. A zircon pinkie ring
4. A beehive hairdo
5. Earth shoes
6. Pipe tobacco that smells so sweet your friends will think you've been smoking a cheerleader
7. Writing thank-you notes on Holiday Inn stationery
8. Pink sponge hair rollers
9. Clear vinyl slipcovers on the living room furniture
10. Zippo lighters that say, "Souvenir of Waycross, Georgia," on the side

You know, non-status seekers are more fun to watch than two hogs in a mud hole.

Never Do These Things

You don't have to go around the block but one time to know that there are some things you can get away with and some things you can't. In the public interest, I have decided to tell you a few things that you should never, ever do:

Never tell Wilt Chamberlain a joke about a tall, black man.

Never order barbecue at a restaurant that serves anything else.

Never make a bank deposit while wearing a ski mask.

Never date a girl who has a fungus named after her.

Never sit on clear, vinyl slipcovers while naked.

Never send a white sport coat to the cleaners with a Hershey bar in the pocket.

Never wear a tie with the Ayatollah's picture on it.

Never ask an antique dealer, "What's new?"

Never wear earrings to a Klan rally.

Never carry an automatic weapon to the airport.

Never sneeze while the dentist is drilling.

Never use a hair dryer in the shower.

Never tell Dolly Parton that she has her water wings on backwards.

Never buy a ticket to an Elvis concert.

Never heat leftover spaghetti in the clothes dryer. (It won't taste too bad, but the lint is murder.)

Never shave your eyelids.

Never try to panhandle a Hari Krishna.

Never buy a toupee from a veterinarian.

Never give permission for your daughter to accompany a football team — anywhere.

Never have a picnic in a chicken house.

Never offer a shrimp to an armed midget.

Never wear flip-flops to a rodeo.

Never arm wrestle a patient in an intensive care unit.

Never sneeze the day after you had a face lift.
Never wear a Flip Wilson T-shirt to a Klan rally.
Never buy wine by the bucket.
Never hang adult shoes from your rear-view mirror.
Never use an electric typewriter in the bathtub.
Never set fire to your eyebrows.
Never date a girl named Walter.
Never wear a suit made out of Tupperware.
Never buy a pacemaker from a door-to-door salesman.
Never swallow with tacks in your mouth.
Never enroll your wife and girlfriend in the same karate class.
Never invest money in a DeSoto dealership.
Never get into a Jacuzzi with the Elephant Man.
Never let your daughter date a man named Igor.
Never get a tattoo on your face.
Never drink from an open fire extinguisher.
Never wear spike heels if your name is Fred.

As I've said before, if you don't do these things, there's no guarantee that you will become healthy, wealthy, or wise. But I firmly believe that by *not* doing these things, you can stay out of a bunch of trouble.

Painless Suicide?

There's a new book out in France. Now, I know you're gonna think I'm kidding, but it's one of the hottest sellers on the French book market. It's called *One Hundred Ways to Commit Suicide Painlessly*.

Well, I have decided to counter that painless suicide book with one of my own. I'm going to list ways to knock yourself off with a great deal of pain. I've already come up with a few, and I can promise you that, if you give these a try, you will discover a very painful way to commit suicide.

For instance, tell a group of Hell's Angels that their mamas' flea collars have expired.

Or, nominate Jane Fonda for Imperial Wizard at a Ku Klux Klan rally.

Frequent a restaurant that specializes in day-old chicken salad.

When you want to get high, inhale glue; not the fumes, the glue.

Use your electric toothbrush in the shower.

Bob for apples in your piranhas' fish tank.

Suggest to your wife that she get a distemper shot.

I doubt if a book on how to kill yourself with a great deal of pain will ever sell, 'cause many folks are just dumb enough to figure it out for themselves.

Things I'd like to See

We all have our hidden desires, but mine may be a little different from most folks'. For example, here are a few of the things I'd like to see:

I'd like to see Donna Reed belch.
I'd like to see Rosalynn Carter dip snuff.
I'd like to see Miss Lillian knee Billy.
I'd like to see Ronald Reagan flat-foot over a vat of Geritol.
I'd like to see Robert Young drink a *real* cup of coffee.
I'd like to see Jimmy Carter have his teeth cleaned by Earl Schib.
I'd like to see Farrah Fawcett sweat.
I'd like to see Dolly Parton on a trampoline. (Talk about perpetual motion!)
I'd like to see Queen Elizabeth in a mud-rasslin' contest with Walter Cronkite.
I'd like to see Fidel Castro in a successful suicide attempt.
I'd like to see Liberace in a fist fight.
I'd like to see Orson Bean disappear.
I'd like to see Rula Lenska in a crew cut.
I'd like to see Ronald McDonald named in a paternity suit.
I'd like to see a commercial about a coffee that's *not* mountain grown in the Andes. I'd like to see one about coffee grown on the edge of a swamp just outside of Tupelo, Mississippi.
I'd like to see a commercial about a laxative that's not gentle. The announcer would say, "It works fast, but it will dang near kill you."
I'd like to see Lassie chase cars.
I'd like to see John Philip Sousa make a comeback. Not his music, but John Philip Sousa.
I'd like to see somebody invent a stainless steel shoelace that would never break.
I'd like to see Danny Thomas be arrogant.

I'd like to see a group of winos do all the beer commercials. I'm tired of all these rich, clean-cut athletes stealing the show. Let's turn beer commercials over to folks who have devoted their lives to drinking beer.

I'd like to see everybody in America smile more, because I believe sunshine is good for your teeth.

Vacations

There are many books and pamphlets around telling you what to do on your vacation. But I'm of the opinion that it is just as important to know what *not* to do on vacations.

In my never-ending effort to make your life more enjoyable, the following is a list of things you should never do on vacations:

Never visit your in-laws.

Never spend your vacation in Hartsville, Alabama.

Never spend your vacation trying to break the world record for passing kidney stones.

Never plan your vacation around a bank robbery.

Never take a mule trip to Antarctica.

Never accept an all-expense-paid trip to Wehunt, West Virginia.

Never wear Bermuda shorts and flip-flops to New Guinea.

Never go into a crowded fire station and holler "Movie!"

If you plan to drive on your vacation, never take a goat along with you.

Never take the Elephant Man with you to a nudist convention.

And last, but not least, if you're planning a motor trip, always take your car.

If you will follow these few simple rules, there's a slight chance you might survive your next vacation.

... Test

... ever gone to work feeling fine and then had somebody tell you that you didn't look well? Suddenly, you actually begin to feel bad, and your whole day is ruined.

It occurred to me that there should be some way to tell if perhaps you might have some medical problem without having to go in for a physical. Therefore, I have put together a list of things that may indicate some medical problem:

You may have a medical problem if your eyebrows fall out.

You may have a medical problem if you are taking communion on Sunday morning, and the clergyman in charge crosses himself . . . and you know you are in a Presbyterian Church.

You should definitely get a checkup if you discover that your navel has disappeared.

You may have a medical problem if you faint at the sight of empty buttermilk glasses.

I would definitely see a doctor if you discover that your ears are interchangeable.

You may have medical problems if it hurts your tongue when you say "Cleveland."

You may need to see your doctor if you enjoy eating Zenith clock radios.

Now, this may not be a sure-fire guide to health and happiness, but it's kind of like chicken soup. What could it hurt?

Buying a House

With the price of houses soaring higher than ever before, and with more and more young married people trying to buy their first house, it occurred to me that somebody should compile a list of things to watch out for, if you're thinking about buying a home.

In my never-ending effort to inform the public, here goes:

Never buy a house that has rice growing in the living room.

Never buy a house next door to a skeet range.

Never buy property inside a leper colony.

Never buy a house from a man who raises seals in his basement.

Never buy a house that has simulated bathrooms.

Never buy a house with a cardboard fireplace.

Never buy a house with total-electric commodes.

Never buy a house with a pigeon roost in the kitchen.

Never buy a house from a real estate agent wearing a ski mask.

Never buy a house with stretch marks on the walls.

Never buy a house with skid marks on the carpet.

I don't know if these little tips will help you buy a house or not. As a matter of fact, with the interest rates as high as they are, I'm not sure anything will help you.

You've Had Enough

With all the publicity about drunken driving, you'd think that people would have figured out by now that it's not a smart thing to do.

I'm not going to browbeat you about drinking and driving, but I will offer you some guidelines, so you will know when you've had too much to drink:

You know you've had too much to drink when you strike a match and light your nose.

You know you've had too much to drink when you pick up your roll and butter your chin.

You know you've had too much to drink when you realize you're the only one in the clothes dryer.

You know you've had too much to drink when you suggest that everyone stand up and sing the national budget.

You know you've had too much to drink when you have been swimming for an hour and suddenly realize that your host doesn't have a pool.

You know you've had too much to drink when you open your eyes and hear someone say, "Call a priest."

You know you've had too much to drink when you realize your foot is sticking out of your fly.

You know you've had too much to drink when you tell your favorite joke to a closet door.

You know you've had too much to drink when you propose marriage to your best friend's beagle.

You know you've had too much to drink when you're sitting at the dinner table and ask your hostess to pass a bedpan.

You know you've had too much to drink when you realize you're using your dishwater for a chaser.

Just a few helpful hints to keep you out of the drunk tank.

Barbecue Standards

Barbecue holds a special place in my heart. It is more important to me than my collection of Tennessee Ernie Ford's greatest gospel hits. It's more important to me than my autographed picture of King Farouk. I tell you all this because I'm genuinely worried about the current state of barbecue in this great country.

Barbecue restaurants are springing up all over, with absolutely no regard for tradition. I, therefore, have come up with a list of guidelines that should be required for barbecue joints. If anybody tries to open up without following these guidelines, the police should be called on 'em at once.

1. They should serve only pork barbecue. Anyone who sells beef barbecue has hairy thighs and ain't right with the Lord.
2. A true barbecue joint must have at least one religious slogan on the walls.
3. If they don't serve Brunswick stew, the owner should be beaten severely with a nine-iron till he does serve Brunswick stew.
4. Any barbecue joint worth its Tabasco should have at least one waitress named Roxy.
5. Never order barbecue at a restaurant that serves anything else.
6. A true barbecue joint should serve only sweet tea; anybody who serves unsweetened tea generally carries pictures of known communists in their billfolds.

I know not what course others may take, but I stand with the late Rufus Moon, who once said, "Pass the loaf bread, Leon."

Child Psychology

I have just finished reading a magazine story by a psychiatrist with a lot of letters behind his name. He was writing about children and how we should raise them.

I'm always a little suspicious of folks who have pat formulas for anything, especially about raising children. They always overlook one simple fact— all children are different; therefore, what will work with one child won't work with another.

This article said that any form of harsh punishment should be avoided, and it went on to list five or six acceptable kinds of punishment. But it overlooked the most obvious means known to mankind to discourage bad behavior in children. It overlooked the method that has been working for countless generations.

It's a simple matter. You look the child in the eye and, with all the sincerity you can muster, say, "Darling, if you ever do that again, Soap Salley will get you." The child then will say, "Who is Soap Salley?" And in a calm, rational voice, you explain that Soap Salley is an ugly old hag of a woman who makes soap out of bad children.

If that doesn't work, you might want to go to what we call phase two, where you discuss in some detail the Boogie Man.

History probably will prove that Soap Salley and the Boogie Man will work in the majority of cases, but if that should fail, you may try the ultimate: Call a contractor and ask him to give you an estimate on building a good, old-fashioned shed out behind your house.

Despicable Things

Will Rogers once said, "I never met a man I didn't like." Now, that sounds good on the face of it, and ole Will got a lot of mileage out of that line. But what's so bad about not liking someone or something? You show me a person who doesn't dislike someone or something, and I'll show you a person without any taste.

Since I am a man of taste, I have prepared a list of things that I not only dislike, but despise. It's a long list, but a good one:

I despise snakes, spiders, and sticky stuff, bleeding hearts and hard hearts, rutabagas and banks that bounce checks, limp bacon, and boring books. I despise things that go bump in the night and fanatics.

I despise phones that ring on Saturday morning, machinery that won't work, and okra that ain't fried. I despise Coke in a can, cold grits, and reformers. I don't like pious people, crooked politicians, waiting in line or bureaucrats.

I despise Brunswick stew in a styrofoam bowl, T-shirts with dirty words on 'em, people who always pick up the check, and people who never pick up the check.

I despise dogs in the garbage and know-it-alls, flat tires, traffic, turnips, tobacco juice, the IRS, loud music, and pain. I also despise all dogs that slobber.

If you disagree with any of these, I understand.

The Truth Hurts

Time has proven that it is very difficult to get through life without telling lies. I guess that's O.K. as long as they don't hurt anybody, but I've noticed a trend that I don't think is healthy — lying to children. I think children can stand the truth and should be given large doses of it.

Three or four years ago, I was in a dentist's office. My son was waiting to have his teeth cleaned, and I was waiting to drive him home.

The door opened and in walked a lady holding the hand of a beautiful little four-year-old boy. He was not crying, but you could tell by the look of fear and dread in his face that this was not his first trip to the dentist. You could also tell that if anyone said the wrong thing to him, he was going to cry his eyes out.

The mother sat down and he fearfully crawled up into her lap, trying to find some comfort there.

I'm a sucker for children, especially if they are going to cry, so I leaned over and said, "Hi, what's your name?" "Jimmy," he whispered. I started to talk to him about "Gilligan's Island" and Captain Kangaroo. I asked him if he wanted to see me do some magic tricks — all children love magic. I did a few sleight-of-hand tricks, and the first thing I knew, he was all smiles and wanted to see some more tricks. He was out of his mother's lap and into my lap and having the time of his life.

About that time, my son came out, and it was time for us to leave. I put Jimmy back into his mother's lap, and I could see the gratitude in her face. Before I left, I bent over and took Jimmy's now-smiling face in my hands. I said, "Jimmy, in a few minutes they are going to come out here, take you by the hand, and lead you in to the dentist. When you get in there, the nice dentist is going to put you in a great, big chair. Jimmy, when that happens, no matter what anybody says or does, don't open your mouth." He said, "Yes, sir."

I turned and walked out. I don't know what was wrong with Jimmy's mama, but it looked like she went into some kind of coma or something.

Yes siree, nothing wrong with telling other people's children the truth.

Crime Signals

With crime sweeping the nation, it's important that we recognize some of the warning signs that generally show up before a crime is committed. If you will be alert and ever-vigilant, you will avoid being a victim of a crime. Following are some danger signals you should watch for:

Be suspicious if you notice that guy in front of you in line is wearing a ski mask.

Suspect trouble if you notice the hitchhiker you just picked up is carrying an M-16.

Be careful, if the guy sitting beside you in the movies suddenly puts his arm around you and starts to sing "Some Enchanted Evening" in your ear.

Be vigilant if you notice that the Girl Scout selling cookies at your door has a beard and a tattoo that says, "Born To Raise Hell."

Be suspicious if you go into a whiskey store and find the employees lying on the floor, nude.

Never lend a stranger your checkbook, and never buy gold bullion from a guy driving a laundry truck.

Just a few tips from *Ludlow's Handbook of Crime Prevention.*

Contemplations, Condemnations, and Consolations

Stray Dogs

I can't count the number of happy hours I have spent with dogs, all kinds of dogs — purebred, puppies, mutts, long-haired, short-haired. You name it; if it has four legs and barks, I've owned it, played with it, enjoyed it, and, most importantly, loved it.

Dogs give a lot and don't ask for much. They need food, water, a safe home, and lots of love, and that's pretty much it.

I guess it's obvious that I not only love dogs, but I also have a lot of respect for them. That's why I was so shocked and upset by a news story I read about a small town in Massachusetts. The town council passed a shoot-to-kill ordinance on stray dogs.

Now, don't get me wrong, I'd be the first one to say that dogs cannot be allowed to run loose. They form packs and can be dangerous. But I disagree with their solution.

So, maybe, just maybe, I have come up with an alternative. Why not pass a shoot-to-wound ordinance on the owners of these dogs? The dogs don't know any better, but the owners do. I wonder how many owners you'd have to shoot before the problem was solved? I guess about one.

Prison Rights

I have noticed in the last few years that some folks in this country have mixed up two words rather badly. They are simple, everyday words, and folks should be aware of the difference in their meanings, but apparently they aren't. The words are *rights* and *privileges*, and they don't mean the same thing at all.

The confusion about these words was brought home to me the other day while I was watching a newscast on TV. A group of convicts was holding some hostages in a prison riot, and the spokesman kept screaming and hollering about their rights. You could tell right off that this old boy didn't know the difference between rights and privileges. I hope someday he reads this book, 'cause I'm about to tell him the difference.

I think everybody knows what a privilege is: That's something we are allowed to do, either by society, or by our boss, or by somebody like that. I think the mix-up comes with the word *rights*. So for the convict who was kind of mixed up, let me give a few examples:

To have color television in prison is a privilege.

To be able to run a convenience store and not be robbed of your hard-earned money, by a punk too lazy to work, is a right.

To have longer recreational periods in prison is a privilege.

To walk the streets safely, without being mugged at night, is a right.

To be able to wear civilian clothes in prison is a privilege.

To be able to sleep safely in your own home is a right.

You know, I'm not surprised that the convict spokesman had these words mixed up. If he had known the difference, chances are he wouldn't have been in prison in the first place.

Possums

I consider the possum to be one of the South's greatest products. I don't know why I like them so much, 'cause they're not good for much of anything. They're not fit to eat, no matter how you fix 'em. And they don't make good pets; they're surly, slow, and awkward.

Maybe it goes back to my love for Pogo, probably the world's most famous possum. Or maybe I just feel sorry for them.

Now, you may find that strange, that somebody could feel sorry for a possum. But I have felt for a long time that possums, as a species, are suicidal. If you don't believe that, just check the highways sometime. Possums are forever jumping in front of cars.

I think I know why they're suicidal, and I don't blame them a bit. It's because they have nothing to look forward to.

They can't look forward to marriage, because when the time comes, the only thing they can marry is another possum. Think about that for a second.

They can't look forward to having babies, because all of their babies are going to be possums.

And would your life be worthwhile, if all of your close friends and associates were possums? Imagine, if you will, going to a Rotary Club Meeting and having a possum as the guest speaker. Imagine electing a possum to public office — naw, I ain't gonna say it, because the obvious is rarely funny.

Cocaine

I was shocked when the headlines screamed out at me, "NFL Stars Admit to Expensive Cocaine Habits." The press jumped on the story like a duck on a June bug, and everybody had something to say about it.

The coaches said they were shocked and would do whatever was necessary to stop cocaine use on their teams.

The sports columnists said it was shocking and that an investigation should be conducted.

Some NFL players spoke out and said that only a small number of players were involved, that most players would never touch cocaine. They said they resented the fact that the majority of the players were taking the rap for the actions of only a few bad players.

They all had something to say, but they all overlooked the most important issue. They all overlooked a sad, simple fact: The children are watching. God, help 'em.

Southern Limitations

Being a native son of the South, I am fiercely proud of the fact that I am a bona-fide, card-carrying, grit-dipping, son of these red clay hills. I also recognize, and accept, the fact that being a native son of Dixie Land means I'm subject to certain limitations. There are, after all, some things that Southerners are not supposed to do.

For example, Southerners should never do any ice skating; not only do we look silly, but it's not healthy. Southerners have weak ankles. This condition is caused by a lifetime of riding in pickup trucks, square dancing, and generally kicking up our heels.

Southerners should never compose operas. There are a couple of reasons for this, one of which is that very few of us can speak Italian, let alone sing it. Besides, I'm not sure how opera lovers would accept arias about trains, prisons, and drinking beer.

Southerners also should never write symphonies. Can't you just imagine a symphony for the banjo?

Southerners should never eat lamb. If God had meant for us to have lamb chops, he never would had invented pigs.

And Southerners never should be granted audiences with royalty, because invariably they will refer to the Queen Mother as the Queen Mama, and that's very embarrassing.

Being a Southerner surely has its limitations, but all in all, it's worth it.

The Water Department

LUDLOW:	Hello, I'd like to speak to someone about my water bill.
OPERATOR:	Do you have an account with us?
LUDLOW:	Do what?
OPERATOR:	Do you charge your water?
LUDLOW:	No, actually, I buy it by the glass and always pay cash.
OPERATOR:	Don't get smart, sir!
LUDLOW:	If I was smart, I wouldn't be on the phone with you; I'd be out digging a well.
OPERATOR:	Don't be sarcastic, sir. Please state your business.
LUDLOW:	I do a radio show and write books.
OPERATOR:	Do what?
LUDLOW:	Look, lady, all I want to do is talk to someone about my water bill.
OPERATOR:	I'll connect you with Mr. Frebish.
FREBISH:	Frebish!
LUDLOW:	I want to talk to you about this outrageous bill I received.
FREBISH:	I'll be glad to help you, sir. What is your meter number?
LUDLOW:	I beg your pardon?
FREBISH:	We file by meter number, and I'm afraid I can't pull your file without your meter number.
LUDLOW:	O.K., I'll play your game. Where do I find my meter number?
FREBISH:	Why, where else, sir — on your meter, of course.
LUDLOW:	It's not written on my bill?
FREBISH:	Don't be an imbecile; why would we put your meter number on your bill?
LUDLOW:	O.K., I give up; where is my meter?

FREBISH:	Why, buried in your front yard, of course.
LUDLOW:	Look, Frebish, I can't get down on my belly and check my meter number. It's raining cats and dogs outside.
FREBISH:	Then why did you call?
LUDLOW:	I called to talk about my bill.
FREBISH:	Very well, sir. What is your meter number?
LUDLOW:	Look, fella, I don't know my meter number, but just answer me one question. Don't you think a hundred and eighty-six thousand dollars for one month's water is a trifle high?
FREBISH:	Sir, I wouldn't be able to comment on that without your meter number.

I'd like to tell you the rest of the conversation, but I'm pretty busy. Anybody know how to dig a well?

The American Pie

The first time I heard it, President Kennedy said it. He said, "Ask not what your country can do for you, ask rather what you can do for your country." I've heard since then that it was not original with President Kennedy, but original or not, it makes me feel proud every time I hear it.

There are many such quotes that make me feel proud and stand a little taller, and a few even make me a little misty-eyed. Quotes like, "Give me liberty or give me death," and "I shall return," or "My only regret is that I have but one life to give for my country."

You don't hear these quotes anymore. They have been replaced with quotes like, "Hell, no, we won't go," and the one that makes the least sense of all, the one that always amazes me when I hear some uninformed fool — be he a private citizen or an elected official — say it: "We want our share of the American Pie."

That's pitiful when you stop and think about it, because what they really mean is, "I want the government to *give* me a piece of the American pie." The unfortunate fact of the matter is that the government doesn't have a pie, because it doesn't produce any of the ingredients.

The government doesn't grow apples or sugar cane or flour. I will admit, as some folks say, that the government has a lot of crust, but that's a different recipe.

Let me tell you how you get a piece of the American pie: You get up every Monday morning and you go to work, and you start earning the apples, the sugar, and the flour. The first thing you know, you've got yourself a delicious, hot apple pie.

If you're willing to produce the ingredients, you can even have pie a la mode in the United States of America.

It tastes a lot better when you furnish the ingredients, but just remember — it all starts first thing Monday morning.

Raiding Party

I read recently that thieves made a raid on the home of the late General William T. Sherman — the one who was careless with matches. About one hundred items were taken from the two-story, brick house, which is now a museum owned by the state of Ohio.

I was shocked to read that the Sherman family silver was stolen. I understand that the beautiful silver will be difficult to replace, since it dates all the way back to the Civil War, and historians are not sure where the general got it. Also stolen were five chairs, which were presents from General Grant, and some exquisite candlesticks.

I know what you're thinking. You're thinking old Ludlow is happy 'cause General Sherman's home got ripped-off. Well, let me assure you that I take no pleasure anytime a thief or looter is successful. I find the act despicable, whether the victim is a civilian or a general.

No sir, I take no pleasure in the raid on General Sherman's home, but I'll tell you what does make me happy, since I'm a bona-fide son of these red, clay hills: It makes me happy that I have an airtight alibi the night the General's home was raided.

Wolves for Gun Control

Once upon a time, there was a little ole girl named Red Riding Hood. She was in her room playing Faron Young records one day when her mama came to the door and said, "Red, turn that noise off and get your shoes on. Your Granny just called. Her Social Security check is late, and she needs something good to eat. I told her I would send you over with some sausage and biscuits, and a Tupperware jug full of white gravy."

Well, Red Riding Hood put the food in a market basket, went outside and, to her horror, found that her Kawasaki wouldn't crank. So her mama told her she had to walk, but that she could take the shortcut through the woods.

Red said, "Mama, you gotta be out of your tree. Don't you know there are haints and boogers in them woods, not to mention communists, wolves, and Lord knows what else." Her mama said, "Stop your bellyaching, big mouth, and get the bricks out before I knock you nose in your watch pocket."

What Red didn't know was that a wolf was hiding behind a chinaberry tree and heard all this, so he cut a trail to grandma's house, hit her in the head with a tire tool, and hid her behind the chifforobe.

About that time, the wolf heard Red coming down the road, so he put on granny's gown and bonnet and jumped into bed. Red walked into the room, and the wolf said, "Welcome, child." Red said, "What's this 'child' jive? If you're my granny, then I'm Burl Ives."

The wolf jumped out of the bed and said, "I'm going to eat you up." Red reached down in her market basket, pulled out a .44 magnum, and shot him between his slimy green eyes.

And that, funseekers, explains why a recent survey showed that most wolves favored gun control.

The Dummies

The older I get, the more I'm convinced that the world is full of dummies. Let me tell you about a group of dummies that even you might fall into.

This particular group of dummies tries to make the world think they love their babies. Yes sir, they make a big show about how much they love them. They turn the spare room into a nursery, and the dummy mama starts knitting booties for the new baby.

Dummy mama is also careful to go to the doctor once a month to make sure her pregnancy is coming along. Dummy daddy is busy thinking about names for the baby, and what college baby should attend.

Finally the big day comes, and God gives a beautiful, healthy baby to these two dummies. Now their show of love *really* begins. Dummy daddy hands out cigars, and dummy mama gets busy making formula and washing diapers.

These two dummies take this beautiful baby to the pediatrician to get him every conceivable innoculation known to medical science.

And then these dummies leave the doctor's office with a baby they claim to love, get into their car, and let the child stand up in the front seat. They put the baby in a position where even a small accident can kill, scar, or mutilate the child they claim to love. Now, that's dumb!

These dummies should know that, outside of birth defects, auto accidents are the leading cause of mental retardation in children.

If you let your baby, regardless of its age, stand up or even get in the car without wearing a seat belt, you're a dummy. If it bothers you to hear me say that, do something about it. Even if you won't buckle up, make sure your kids do. Don't be a dummy.

What Do You See, Nurses?

Mother's Day is becoming more and more of a family holiday, where we go to the lake or have a cookout. But while families are out having fun, many older mothers sit in nursing homes with only flowers and Hallmark cards.

The following poem was found among the effects of a patient who died many years ago at the Oxford University Geriatric Service in England. The author is unknown. I want you to read this carefully, and then I want you to decide what you'll be doing next Mother's Day:

What Do You See, Nurses?

What do you see, nurses, what do you see?
What are you thinking, when you look at me?
A crabby old woman, not very wise,
Uncertain of habit, with faraway eyes,
Who dribbles her food and makes no reply,
When you say in a loud voice, "I do wish you would try!"
Who seems not to notice the things that you do,
And forever is losing a stocking or shoe;
Who, unresisting or not, lets you do as you will,
When bathing and feeding, a long day to fill.
Is that what you're thinking; is that what you see?
Then open your eyes, nurse, you're not looking at me.
I'll tell you who I am, as I sit here so still,
As I drink at your bidding, as I eat at your will.
I'm a small child of ten, with a father and mother,
Brothers and sisters, who love one another.
A young girl of sixteen, with wings on her feet,
Dreaming that soon now, a lover she'll meet.
A bride soon of twenty, my heart gives a leap,
Remembering the vows that I promised to keep.
At twenty-five now, I have young of my own,
Who need me to build a secure, happy home.

A woman of thirty, my young now grow fast,
Bound to each other with ties that should last.
At forty, my young sons, near grown, will be gone,
But my man stands beside me, to see I don't mourn.
At fifty, once more babies play around my knee;
Again we know children, my loved one and me.
Dark days are upon me — my husband is dead;
I look in the future and shudder with dread.
For my young are all busy, rearing young of their own,
And I think of the years, of the love I have known.
I'm an old woman now, and nature is cruel;
It's her jest to make old age look like a fool.
The body, it crumbles, grace and vigor depart;
There is now a stone where I once had a heart.
But inside this old carcass, a young girl still dwells,
And now and again, my battered heart swells.
I remember the joys, I remember the pain,
And I am loving and living life over again.
I think of the years, all too few, gone too fast,
And accept the stark fact — nothing can last.
So open your eyes, nurses, open and see,
Not a crabby old woman — look closer, see me.

Heartaches

I've decided to do a little speculation with my tongue planted firmly in my cheek.

Wouldn't it be funny if we found out that heart surgery is all a scam, by the doctors and hospitals, to make money?

Now, common sense will tell you that it is impossible to take somebody's heart out of their body, do something to it, and then put it back. Doctors admit that they can't cure the common cold, but they would have us believe that they can operate on a fellow's heart.

Naw, it's just a money-making scheme. Once they get the sucker in the operating room and put him to sleep, the doctors and nurses take off their surgical masks, break out their Parcheesi board, and play Parcheesi for five or six hours.

When enough time has passed, one of the doctors goes out to the waiting room where the family is gathered, smiles at 'em, and says, "The operation was a great success — Leon is going to be fine. That will be twenty-seven thousand dollars, please."

There's a story going around about this young doctor who was really going to operate. One of the older doctors grabbed his arm and said, "You can't operate on this patient, you young fool! You'd kill him. He has heart trouble."

Now, before all you doctors and hospital administrators start to write me letters, let me say that I'm just kidding. You do great and wonderful work, and mankind is in your debt . . . not as much as your patients, but close.

Chain Letters

I've been getting chain letters all of my life. You know, the ones that promise to make you rich, or bring you good luck, or get you into heaven, or have somebody on the list send you four thousand bottles of whiskey.

The other day, however, I received the weirdest chain letter of all. The instructions were very simple: I was to take the name on top of the list, go to that person's house, ring the doorbell, and when the guy answered the door, I was supposed to beat him up.

The letter went on to say that I was then supposed to add my worst enemy's name at the bottom of the list, make twelve copies of the letter, and mail them out.

The letter said that if I followed these simple instructions, I could rest well that night, secure in the knowledge that in the next thirty days, my worst enemy would be beaten senseless three thousand, four hundred and eighty-six times.

The letter closed by saying that in 1941, a Navy ensign broke the chain, and less than thirty days later, the Japanese bombed Pearl Harbor.

I think I'm gonna do it; you can't be too careful about things like this.

Hide-and-Seek

I'm involved in a project that I would like to tell you about. I'm trying to get the Olympic Committee to start a hide-and-seek event. Now, before you laugh, think about it. The Olympic Hide-and-Seek — two teams of expert hide-and-seekers.

I, of course, would be the captain of the American team, and my beloved friend Lardo DuPree would be the co-captain. I would be the captain because I am one of the few adults in the world who remembers the finer points of hide-and-seek. Lardo would be the co-captain 'cause he ain't never won a trophy.

What are my credentials for this prestigious job? Well, I'll tell you. Who else around remembers this: "Bushel of wheat, bushel of rye, who's not ready, holler I?" Or this immortal chant: "Bushel of wheat, bushel of clover, who's not ready, can't hide over?"

As a matter of national pride, we should have an Olympic hide-and-seek team. Can't you see it now? The U.S. versus the Russians in hide-and-seek. Can't you just see me and old Lardo getting that gold medal? Can't you just imagine the U.S. coming up with a new native-American event? I can hardly wait.

I'm not an arrogant man, but I've got to tell you, fun-seekers, there ain't never been a commie-pinko-bedwetter anywhere that I couldn't just wear out in hide-and-seek. You mark my words: If we can get Olympic hide-and-seek, we can send those folks back to Moscow talking to themselves.

Put It Off Till Tomorrow

Did you know there is a National Procrastination Day? That's right. Someone came up with a great idea. I, of course, thought of it first, but didn't do anything about it because I put it off.

I cannot tell you how important this day is to me, 'cause I am the king of procrastinators. Now, I know there are a lot of other folks who think they know something about putting things off. But let me assure you: I am to procrastination what Esther Williams was to wet.

Let me give you a few examples of things that seem perfectly all right to us procrastinators, but seem to bother other folks:

I never have my driver's license renewed in any month that has an R in it.

I eat lunch every day at high three o'clock.

I just mailed Tom Dewey his campaign contribution.

I have garbage in my kitchen older than Wayne Newton.

I just finished Ernest Hemingway's latest novel.

I'm going tomorrow to get my swine flu shot.

I'm opposed to giving away the Panama Canal. I'm going to send a letter of protest tomorrow telling President Carter so.

There are a lot of other things we procrastinators do, but I'll tell you about them in my next book.

Things I Don't Understand

We've talked about this before, the fact that the older you get, the more some things seem to puzzle you. There are just a lot of things going on that I don't understand.

For example, I hate white gumballs — they remind me of Fenamint. I don't understand why I always get a white gumball out of the machine.

I don't understand where fat goes when you lose it.

I don't understand why Dick Tracy never goes home. He's been working on one case or another since about 1934. Near as I can figure, the last time he was at home was sometime just before the Korean War.

I don't understand soccer.

I don't understand why you've got to have a license to fish, but you can drink whiskey without one.

I don't understand why the witch in "Snow White" fools with the poison apple. Why didn't she just buy her a Saturday Night Special, shoot Snow White, and be done with it?

I don't understand why they pay folks to play football. My friends and I used to do it all the time for free.

I don't understand why adults don't play hide-and-seek.

Once Moor, With Feeling

I heard an Englishman on television the other day, and he was just a-fussing about the U.S. involvement in El Salvador. A few minutes later, he changed gears and started raising Cain about the Russians in Afghanistan. Then the next thing I knew, he shot his mouth into overdrive and was talking about the Japanese killing whales.

Now, I don't know if he was right or wrong about the rest of the world, but it looks to me like he would worry about the big English problem before he'd branch out and become an international Dear Abby.

Did you know England has a place called the moors? And nobody is doing anything about it. Let me tell you about the moors; I know all about them because of the movies.

The first thing you need to know about the moors is that nothing good ever happens there. You never hear one Englishman say to another Englishman, "Hey, Basil, let's go out on the moors and shag a few fly balls and get us a Big Orange."

You can go slap from one end of the moors to the next and never see a Dairy Queen, or even a Stuckey's. As a matter of fact, all you ever see is old, worn-out mansions that look like Urban Renewal rejects.

For some reason that I don't understand, people like to walk across the moors. Everybody tries to tell them it's dangerous, but they never listen. You can just look at the moors and tell they are full of haints, ghosts, and boogers, and for some reason, they are always foggy. Not only that, but it is always dark on the moors. It looks to me like the English government ought to do something about the moors and stop worrying about the rest of the world.

I'll tell you one thing: If we had moors in this country, Ralph Nadar would organize a demonstration before you could say Basil Rathbone.

No Children

I read the other day that the population has stopped growing, and that the average family is now smaller than the traditional 2.5 children. The thing that surprised me most was the number of people choosing to be sterilized at very young ages.

Some girls are making that important decision as young as seventeen years old, and more young men than ever before are having vasectomies.

If that's what they want, it's certainly their business, but it makes me sad to think of Halloween without lots of children around. It can be a hassle buying candy and jumping up and down every time the doorbell rings, but it's all worth it the first time you take your own little Spiderman out for his first trick-or-treat.

And who can even imagine Christmas without little children?

Just think how it would be never to know the thrill of seeing your daughter in her first cheerleader uniform, or taking your son for his first haircut.

Having children is a very personal decision and should be made with a lot of thought, but wouldn't it be awful if there were nobody around to spill milk on the floor? Or to kiss you on the cheek with jelly on their mouth? And wouldn't it just be awful if there were nobody in the whole world who called you mama or daddy?

New Car Fever

New car fever is a terrible thing to catch, but I'll tell you something that's even worse — having nightmares about buying new cars.

I dreamed the other night that I bought a new German car. It was shiny, and I loved it. I was driving down the street when this voice came out of the dashboard and said, "Buckle your seat belts." So I buckled up. Then the voice said, "Let me see your papers." I said, "Do what?" The voice said, "You heard me, swine; let me see your papers." I said, "What papers? I don't have any papers." The voice said, "You don't lie to me. We know you have relatives in the Father Land."

I was so upset in my dream that I stopped immediately and traded the German car for a fancy, Polish station wagon.

I was riding down the road in that one and another voice came out of the dashboard and said, "Your fuel is low." I said, "Thank you." Then the voice said, "Do you know how many Americans it takes to change a light bulb?"

I woke up in a cold sweat. Nothing on earth will cure new car fever faster than a good, old-fashioned nightmare.

Job Opportunity

I thought I had misunderstood the television announcer when he said, "More than two hundred young people take their demands for jobs to the downtown streets." I guess the thing that got me the most was the word *demand*. I don't know how anyone can demand a job; that seems to imply that in the United States of America, you have a *right* to a job.

A young man being interviewed on TV was noticeably bitter, and even more noticeably dumb. He said that big business had not done enough to create jobs, and that if they had no jobs, then private corporations should pay this uninformed crowd to perform public service jobs.

Well, that ain't the way it works, gang. Big business has no obligation to you, and neither does small business. But if you've got another minute before you run out to rent another bullhorn, I'll tell you who does have an obligation to get you a job: You do, boopsie.

That's right; I know it sounds strange to a man carrying a picket sign, but it's a fact. The simplest way to get a job is to prepare yourself to make yourself useful to an employer. Then you either get a job created for you, or you take one away from somebody else. That's the way the system works. It's the only way it will work, and all the high sounding, arrogant, naive rhetoric on the face of the earth won't change the facts.

I feel like a man who just wasted a lot of time typing this.

My New Telephone

The most wonderful thing has come into my life — so wonderful that I must share it with you.

We just got new telephones where I work.

Now, before you turn up your nose and say, "Big deal," let me tell you that I ain't talking about no ordinary telephones. I'm talking about the fanciest thing to come on the market since mustard.

This phone does everything a phone is supposed to do and a lot more. It's got a built-in radio, a built-in intercom, and a built-in paging system.

You think that's something, listen to this: My new phone has peddles and you can ride the sucker. It has a microwave oven, so that you sit right at your desk and make cheese toast while you're working. Not only that, but you can use it to make bank deposits or be checked for a hernia.

My new phone will pull a water skier, tutor you in algebra, or give you the words and music to "Who Threw the Overalls in Mrs. Murphy's Chowder?" My new phone can even cure the common cold, gout, and the heartbreak of psoriasis.

Now, you wanna know the big news? The big news is that next week, they're going to teach me how to get an outside line.

I can hardly stand it.

Grounded

I recently learned an important lesson: Never try to save money on airline fares.

I booked a flight on Fred's Airline. I knew I had made a terrible mistake, when I went out to get on the plane and saw a big dent in one of the wings. For some strange reason, I got on the plane, anyway.

I handed my boarding pass to the flight attendant, and she said, "How the hell are you, tubby? My name's Shirley Sleeze, and I'll be your flight attendant."

She was wearing a very strange uniform for a flight attendant: Levis, flip-flops, and an STP T-shirt. I said, "Good morning, Miss Sleeze; where's my seat?" She said, "Just put it anywhere, bucko, we ain't never crowded."

Well, I sat down and was ready to go, but nothing happened. When Shirley brought me my complimentary glass of buttermilk, I asked her what the delay was. She said that there was a mechanical problem.

I sat there for about fifteen minutes more, and then a man came down the aisle wearing cover-alls and a baseball hat that said "Tube Rose Snuff" on the front. I said, "Pardon me, sir; are you the mechanic?" He said, "Naw, I'm the pilot." I asked, "What's the trouble?" He said, "Dead battery. But don't worry; Leon's out now, trying to borrow a set of jumper cables."

As I was getting off the plane, Shirley hollered at me, "Hey, don't go, we've almost got it fixed. Besides, you didn't get your second glass of complimentary buttermilk." I said, "Never mind, Miss Sleeze, there ain't that much buttermilk in the whole world."

Sex Discrimination

I've said it before, and I'll say it again — I'm not equipped to live in this century.

Just about the time I think I've got it figured out, something happens that hits me hard enough to knock the sap out of a chinaberry tree.

A French restaurant in Los Angeles is being sued for sex discrimination for handing out menus with prices to men, while giving out priceless menus to women.

There's this old girl out there in California, and she says she was humiliated and incensed when she took her law partner out to dinner at this restaurant and was handed the priceless menu.

According to the news story, it not only made her mad, but her law partner wasn't tickled, either. So they sued the restaurant and asked for two hundred and fifty dollars in damages and a permanent injunction to end the menu practice.

The man who owns the restaurant is a gentleman named Gerard Ferry, and he says he will continue to use his latest menu with no prices.

I wish I could tell you that this could happen only in California, but the fact of the matter is that this kind of asinine lunacy has spread from the Looney Tunes state to the whole country. It's fine to talk about not discriminating against women, or anyone, because to do so is bad, and every right-thinking person knows and understands this.

But tell me, funseekers, when in the hell is someone going to start worrying about the Gerard Ferrys of the world?

Here is a man who has worked hard to build his business, and now two off-the-wall busybodies are trying to tell him how to run his business. And do you know what turns my stomach? Some judge, who has been eating from the public trough all his life, is going to tell this man what he can and what he can't put on his menu.

I'll bet you Thomas Jefferson is spinning in his grave like a Mix Master at the Pillsbury Bakeoff.

Did You Notice?

I've been accused of having a strange sense of humor, but I don't happen to believe that. Actually, my sense of humor isn't much different from anyone else's; I just notice a lot of things other folks don't notice.

For example, have you noticed that Fred Astaire isn't as agile as he used to be? I think it's hurting his movie career; he hasn't had a starring role in years.

Have you ever noticed that all of Great Britian's political leaders have real heavy accents? I don't know why that is, unless most of the British voters are big Charles Lawton fans. I also have this theory that if you woke up a British prime minister in the middle of the night, he'd talk just like the rest of us.

Another thing I've noticed is that Superman wears his uniform under his suit when he's Clark Kent, but I don't understand what he does with the cape? And what does he do with his glasses when he's Superman?

I guess I didn't notice everything, after all.

Canadian Rats

I recently read an interesting story out of Canada. There's a fellow in Alberta who's an Alcohol Abuse official, and he claims that U.S. country music is driving folks to drink. He says the lyrics and sad tone of many country western tunes are such that listeners are tempted to reach for the bottle.

Among the tunes he cited as examples are Tom Wait's version of, "I Don't Have a Drinking Problem, Except When I Can't Get Drunk;" Johnny Cash's "Put the Bottle on the Table, Let Me Drink 'Til I'm Not Able;" and Merle Haggard's album titled "Back to the Barroom."

Now, it seems to me that anybody would know that singing don't make you drink — drinking makes you sing. Lord knows, if country/western music would make you drink, there wouldn't be a sober person alive south of Richmond, Virginia.

As a matter of fact, I think many country songs make a strong social comment against alcohol abuse, like Willie Nelson's "I Gotta Get Drunk and I Sure Do Dread It." I'm sure that song has stopped a lot of folks from opening that next Pabst Blue Ribbon.

And who could ever forget the lesson to be learned from that haunting refrain, "I Was Drunk the Day My Mama Got Out of Prison?" And let's not forget Webb Pierce's immortal classic, "There Stands the Glass."

Seems to me that if the government officials in Canada would stick to giving diet soft drinks to rats and let country music take its course, we could wipe out winos in our own time.

It's Bad for You

As you read the papers about what's good for you and what will kill you, you begin to realize that all of the things you grew up loving are really bad for you. I'm not talking about whiskey and cigarettes; folks have known for years that they are bad for you. I'm talking about good, wonderful, wholesome things that suddenly have turned bad for you. Things like white bread.

I love white bread. I adore white bread. If I had been born five hundred years ago, in all likelihood I would have belonged to a cult that worshipped white bread.

Some doctors say that sugar is bad for you, and the health food freaks call it poison. But can you imagine a sugarless life? Imagine growing up in a world with no sugar. Just imagine taking your best girl to the drugstore for a cherry Tab.

Imagine the Saturday Matinee without Tootsie Rolls, Mr. Goodbar, and jujubes. Imagine a birthday party without ice cream and cake. Imagine, if you will, a circus with no cotton candy, or county fairs without candy apples.

I don't know if doing without sugar will make us live longer or not, but it sure would seem longer.

The House We Live In

You know, the human animal is a strange and wonderful thing. Of all God's creatures, he is the one most apt to take a very good situation and work overtime to make it worse. Simplicity seems to bother him; he will strip the landscape of all trees and foliage, and then build a dam to stop flooding.

If he's not satisfied with the time the sun sets, he'll just change it with daylight-saving time. If the fact that Columbus' birthday falls on a Wednesday bothers him, he'll just change it to Monday.

When our founding fathers set down to talk about the Constitution of the United States, they didn't take their job lightly. As a matter of fact, they worked long and hard to come up with that marvelous blueprint for the house we live in. But people continue trying to complicate that old document.

We'll all be going into a voting booth some day soon, and before we do, it might be a good idea to take a quick look at the Constitution of the United States.

It says right up front, plain as a tattoo on a preacher, what it is supposed to do for us. There are five things; no more, just five. They go something like this:

(1.) Establish justice; that means make laws.

(2.) Insure domestic tranquillity; that means have police to keep the peace.

(3.) Provide for the common defense; that means keep a strong national defense.

(4.) Promote the general welfare. Some folks like to leave out the "general," but you can bet your mortgage money that Madison didn't mean food stamps; he meant schools.

(5.) Secure the blessing of liberty for ourselves and our posterity; that means freedom from government oppression for us and for our children, and our children's children.

Five simple things, that's all. Memorize all five, and then listen carefully to politicians' speeches. Any politician who wants to do more than these five things wants to take money away from you to do something he's got no business doing. If nothing else, the son-of-a-gun will sure bear watching.

Television, Rock Music, and ther Wastelands

The New Soap Operas

A while back, I was off from work with a cold. I wasn't deathly sick; I was what you call tolerable, which means you're able to sit up and take nourishment, but not able to go to work. Well, since I was able to sit up, I had a chance to watch some soap operas for the first time in about ten years, and I've got to tell you that soap operas have really changed.

There was a man and a woman on the screen. Their names were Jeffrey and Cynthia. I was sitting in bed with a pillow under my head, Vicks Vapo-Rub on my chest, and Campbell's chicken soup in my stomach, and here's what I heard coming out of the television set:

JEFFREY: Cynthia, my darling, why are you leaving me?

CYNTHIA: Jeffrey, I am leaving you because you tried to set me on fire while I was sleeping.

JEFFREY: I must have been out of my mind. I only did it because you were pregnant by my brother Basil.

CYNTHIA: Who?

JEFFREY: You know, the tall blond doctor, Basil.

CYNTHIA: That's your brother?

JEFFREY: Yes, you remember; he was best man at our wedding.

CYNTHIA: Oh! *That* Basil.

JEFFREY: Please, please don't leave me. If you go, I will kill myself.

CYNTHIA: I must leave you, Jeffrey. You see, I'm not only pregnant with Basil's baby, I'm also pregnant by the New York Jets. I'm a paraplegic, and I am currently suffering from irregularity and the heartbreak of psoriasis.

JEFFREY: Do what?

CYNTHIA: I'm going to kill myself.

JEFFREY: I think you're doing the right thing, but before you do it, tell me . . . the entire New York Jets football team?

CYNTHIA: Yes, plus two guys with their P.R. department, and a midget I met at the will-call window.

You know what I think? I think that sound you're hearing is Ma Perkins turning over in her grave.

Comic Capers

I don't know about you, but I, for one, have always believed that evil should be exposed wherever it exists. There are some things not being discussed by the media which need to be openly discussed, on an adult level, and this may be the place to discuss them.

For example, don't you think that it's high time that Donald Duck invested in a pair of trousers? I don't care about the obviously immoral conduct between Donald and Daisy, but I do think that old-fashioned decency requires that the ill-tempered little duck put on a pair of britches. It's no wonder that Huey, Dewey, and Louie are such unmanageable little hellions, with that perverted duck for an uncle.

And how about the Lone Ranger and Tonto? I mean, I know it's 1983, but what's really going on here in front of our children? A grown man who wears a mask, skin-tight pants, and shoots only silver bullets. (Liberace, cry your eyes out.) And how about that sissy white horse, with the silver saddle, that he always refers to as, "Big Fella." And Tonto — all he ever does is look at him with those big, brown eyes and grunt, "Kemo sabe." God only know's what that means!

How about the Phantom and his purple body suit? Come on, fella, don't you know that kind of perverted behavior went out with Bugler Tobacco?

This brings me to the one I consider to be the most offensive of all — that gutless "Uncle Tom" rat, Mickey Mouse. It's quite obvious to everybody that Mickey is black, but there he sits on his pedestal, while the world passes him by. Did he speak up during the lunch counter sit-ins? Has he ever spent one minute of time trying to help his people? The answer is no. Mickey Mouse, you are a disgrace!

If we're ever going to have any law and order in this country, the first thing we have to do is clean up our comic strips. History will prove that no civilization can long stand whose comic strips are as fouled up as Hogan's goat.

Headlines

Have you noticed how the newspapers you buy in grocery stores and convenience stores always write headlines to grab your attention?

Most of these stories are usually garbage, of course, but the headlines are so intriguing that you just have to buy one of these tabloids to find out the rest of the story. I've always had this mental picture of a guy sitting around trying to think of a provocative headline for one of these newspapers.

Well, with that in mind, I thought to myself, "Ludlow, you could do that and turn a dollar or two at the same time." So I put together some headlines that I'm going to try to sell to some of these national tabloids. See if you could resist buying these headlines:

"Fugitive Hides in a Bread Box for Eight Years."

Or how about, "Now It Can Be Told: Howard Hughes Was My Long-Lost Sister."

Religious news is always big anywhere in the world, and this headline would certainly sell some papers: "Outraged Nun Stomps Sinful Dwarf to Death."

Medical news is also a big attention-getter. Picture these headlines: "Cancer Can Be Cured With Ketchup," or "Three Sure-Fire Ways to Tell When Your Husband Is Dead."

Any headline about a celebrity is a sure winner, if you word it right, like this: "Lady Di Gets Naked Every Day." Or this one: "What Advice Did Burt Reynolds Give to Sal Mineo About Religion?" Or even this one: "For the First Time, Barbra Streisand Tells the True Story About Her Nose."

You know, as good as these headlines are, it's just a shame that they're going to wind up on the bottom of a bird cage.

Scripts Have Changed

I was watching a show on television a while back, about two female New York police officers. This was to be the new dramatic hit of the year.

The show opened up with this lady cop in bed with a civilian of the opposite sex. All either one of them was wearing was a smile. It was a two-hour show, and they used an awful lot of cuss words, and showed an awful lot of flesh.

Well, none of this shocked me much, 'cause I'm a real hard fellow to shock. I have been all around the world; I even spent the night once in Hartsville, Alabama, so you know right off I'm a hard fellow to shock.

But seeing all of this on television made me stop and think how times have changed. I don't know if they've changed for the better or not, but I do know they have changed.

I remember when Rhett Butler told Scarlett that it didn't make no never mind to him what she did. Folks thought it was awful, 'cause he used a four-letter word to tell her.

I remember that when the Thin Man and his wife went to bed, they always used twin beds, and they were always covered from head to toe with pajamas. And when movies showed the bathroom, it never had a commode in it.

Well, now the screen is full of naked folks doing everything from sleeping together to putting up aluminum siding on their house. You can hear just about every four-letter word the mind of man can come up with. And they not only show commodes, they show folks using them.

Maybe it is my imagination, but I think the old movies were much better.

You see, I've seen folks using commodes in real life, and it just ain't very entertaining.

Radio Appreciation

It seems to me that every year the new television shows get stranger and more off-the-wall. I sometimes marvel at the fact that some of them make it as far as their season premiere.

I was reading a story the other night about the coming season. Did you know there's a new situation comedy coming out about a funeral director and his family? It's called "Leave It to Bereaver."

One of the most exciting quiz shows to come along in years is also due out soon; it's called "You Bet Your Mama." If you miss the big question, your mama has to go to work as a scrub woman for the network for the rest of her life. But if you answer the big question correctly, you win Cleveland, Ohio.

This must be a big year for westerns, because there are two new western series scheduled. One is set in Italy; it's called "Who Put Spaghetti in My Saddle Bags?" The other is about a gay Texas Ranger, and it's called "The Lawman Wore Pink."

There is also a spin-off from "Snow White and the Seven Dwarfs." It's about the life and times of the little-known eighth dwarf, who was a sex pervert. The new show is called "Sleezy."

One show that really caught my eye features Allen Funt as host. It's called "This Is Your Wife." Viewers who suspect their wives are running around on them write in, and a camera crew follows her till they catch her going into a motel. Then they film the affair through a one-way glass, and put it on television. If your wife is the guilty one for the week, you get a T-shirt and a quickie Mexican divorce.

And I just can't wait to see the new mini-series about the house of ill repute that's set up in a jumbo jet, that just flies out of town, when the police get ready to raid it. The new show is called, "Gone With the Sin."

You know, the more I read about the new TV shows, the more I appreciate my radio.

Spring *Is Sprung*

I recently received a new magazine in the mail. It was the very first issue, and they wanted me to subscribe.

The name of the magazine was "Spring," and it was all about high-energy living. I found that kind of strange, 'cause all of my life, I've been trying to live using as little energy as possible. That's why I have a car, a dishwasher, and a dryer, all designed to assure me of low-energy living.

The lead article in the magazine was entitled, "How Swedes Keep Fit." Well, since Sweden has the highest suicide rate in the world and the most pornography, I would assume that Swedes keep fit by either making love, or reading about somebody else making love, or killing themselves. I didn't read that article.

The next article was called, "High-Protein Salads You Can Live On." That's kind of dumb, too, at least to me. If all I could have was salads, I wouldn't care if I lived or died.

Another story was called, "A New Technique to Get Your Agenda Rolling." Now, I don't know about you, but anytime my agenda starts rolling, I take two Rolaids or some Pepto-Bismol, and it quietens right down.

The last story was about natural healing for women. I guess that's opposed to *unnatural* healing. I wonder what unnatural healing is?

In any event, I wish the folks at *Spring* magazine success with their venture, but I think I'll stick with *Colliers*.

Hairy Commercials

I may be wrong, but it seems to me that a lot of today's television commercials are written by Madison Avenue to be shown only to chimpanzees.

There's one in particular that just tears me up. For some reason, they show this one only late at night, or at two or three o'clock in the morning.

The commercial opens with a bunch of folks playing volly-ball in the sand. The announcer says, "Meet Paul Krause, hard-charging defense man for the Minnesota Vikings. Volley-ball keeps him young, and girls help, too."

At that point, the camera cuts to a bunch of girl spectators, who all look like Dolly Parton with a chest cold. The announcer continues. "But Paul has what some people consider a handicap: He's bald." Then the announcer goes on to say that Paul wears a wig, and he tells you where to buy one just like it.

Well, in the first place, I never heard of Paul Krause. But that's O.K., because he probably never heard of me, either. In the second place, if playing volleyball in front of girls with big gazoongas would keep you young, then a volleyball court would be harder to rent than a fifty-pound bag of uranium at King Hardware.

I think the thing that bothers me most is that they never show a close-up of Paul Krause wearing his wig. The only reason I can figure for that is, he must have a dead tomcat on top of his head.

Gird Your Loins

I was watching an old English movie the other night. You know, one of those made in the thirties with a lot of fog and sword fighting. These two old boys were getting ready to fight, and one of 'em hollered out to the other one, "Gird your loins, varlet!"

Well, after he hollered that, they got into the dangest scrap you have ever seen in your entire life, and after a few minutes of fighting, one of them killed the other one. The only reason I can figure why he won, was he must have had his loins girded better than the loser.

You show me a fellow who's good at loin girding, and I'll show you a winner every time.

Shortly after I saw this English movie, I dropped by my favorite beer joint, the Château Switchblade. And wouldn't you know it, there at the bar was Snake Burnett, the meanest man who ever lived. He was having a few cold ones and telling everybody what a great president Barry Goldwater would have made.

The bartender said, "You've had enough to drink. Now, stop all that political talk, or I'm going to throw you out." Well, bless Pat, I don't believe I ever saw a man get quite as mad as Snake did. He stepped back from the bar and screamed at the top of his lungs, "You'll throw no one out! Gird your loins, varlet!"

The police came and locked up Snake. I guess like everything else, loin girding ain't what it used to be.

Silver Screen Injustice

I really enjoy the old movies. I grew up watching them, and I still enjoy catching one on the late show. But did you ever notice how much injustice they had in old movies? I mean, take the Lone Ranger and Tonto. Now, the Ranger called him his faithful Indian companion, but if you look closely, you will see that Tonto and the Lone Ranger had a master/servant relationship. No matter what Tonto wanted to do, he was never allowed to do it.

Tonto would say, "Look like good place to camp, Lone Ranger," and the Ranger would say, "No, Tonto, we'll go on to the mesa and camp." Or he would say, "Tonto go with you, kemo sabe," and the Ranger would say, "No, Tonto, you wait here." A definite master/servant relationship.

Talking about injustices, take Tarzan. Did you ever notice how, when the natives captured him and tied him to a big pole, they would go into a powwow to decide what to do with ole Tarzan? And you know, they always decided to give him the death penalty. Sometimes they decided to burn him alive, and sometimes they decided to feed him to the lions or crocodiles, but they never gave him ninety days, or thirty days, or even a heavy fine. He always got the death penalty. That's strange.

Gabby Hayes is another great example. Why did they always make him gray? I don't mean just his hair and beard; I mean they made his face gray, his clothing gray, and his horse gray. He was the only sidekick in Hollywood who shot a gray pistol, and when he cooked for Hopalong Cassidy, he cooked gray food in a gray pot.

Old Hollywood was full of injustice, but at least they kept their clothes on.

Music Review

As one of the South's foremost music critics, it fell my task to review the Rolling Stones concert at the fabulous Fox Theater, in Atlanta, Georgia, a couple of years ago.

Based on that experience, I have a few observations I would like to pass on to you. For one, Mick Jagger does not spend enough money on plastic surgery. I am trying to say, as gently as possible, that Mick Jagger is unattractive. No, I guess what I am trying to say is that he is unpleasant to look upon. No, I guess what I'm really trying to say is that last Thursday on highway seventy-eight, between Loganville and Splitsilk, I saw a dead possum that was better looking than Mick Jagger.

Now, I know the poor thing can't help what he looks like, but with the price of sacks being what it is, there's just no reason to put the public through the trauma of looking at Mick Jagger.

Observation number two: Mick Jagger's lead guitar player is uglier than Mick Jagger. And not only that, but he seems to be in some kind of trance, to boot. He just stands there, with enough hair to stuff a mattress, and stares out into space like he's expecting something to come after him, and he ain't sure what.

Then there was their music; it was loud. Then there was the theater; it was packed. Then there was the crowd; they were tickled. Then there was me; I was lonesome for Glenn Miller, Tommy Dorsey, and the Modernaires with Paula Kelley.

Good Guys and Bad Guys

I have finally discovered why it is so difficult to live in the 1980s. It's so simple, I don't know why I didn't think of it before. Life is more difficult now because you can't tell the good guys from the bad guys. And by golly, that's important.

Just a few short years back, when you went to a movie, you could always tell the good guys from the bad guys, especially in the old westerns. It seemed that Hollywood had set up some sort of good guy/bad guy guidelines, and nobody ever went outside these guidelines.

Do you remember? Bad guys wore black, and good guys wore white. There were only three exceptions: Hopalong Cassidy, the Durango Kid, and Lash LaRue. The good guys were always cleanshaven, and the bad guys always had a three-day growth of beard. Good guys could sing or not sing — it was optional. On the other hand, bad guys were never ever allowed to sing or play any type of musical instrument.

Good guys always rode great horses, like palaminos or paints, or snow-white albinos. Bad guys were never ever allowed to ride a name-brand horse. In the barroom fights, good guys were never allowed to pick up chairs or bottles to use as weapons. The bad guys were allowed to use anything they could get their hands on. Good guys were allowed to have friends who said funny things. The bad guys' friends were only allowed to say things like, "Yes, boss."

Don't you wish it were like that now? Think how easy it would be on election day, if we could just tell the good guys from the bad guys.

Surviving the Eighties

It seems to me that every way I turn in the 1980s, I get disillusioned. I think it's because the advertising folks have promised me so much with their little slogans, that it's easy to be disappointed.

Let me tell you what has happened to me in the last month or so. It all started when I went to buy an airline ticket and found out, to my horror, that they were not ready when I was. I went to the next counter, bought a ticket on the Friendly Skies, and the plane got hijacked.

I made a cup of coffee; not only was it not good to the last drop, but the whole cup tasted like somebody had boiled a flip-flop in it. I bought a box of cereal that said it had two scoops of raisins in the box; it did — no cereal, just two scoops of raisins. I dropped my wristwatch into a blender, and guess what — it quit ticking.

I almost strangled on one of those tiny little tea leaves. I stopped at a convenience store to get some antacid tablets; but when the guy behind the counter found out I couldn't spell relief, he wouldn't sell 'em to me. And my final disappointment for the month was when I found out my grocer couldn't care less if I squeezed the toilet paper.

I'm sure I am not emotionally prepared to survive in the 1980s.

Confusing Commercials

I watch television for entertainment, but every once in a while I see something that just about worries me to death. I have racked my brain for hours trying to figure out two current TV commercials.

For instance, I still haven't figured out how a five-day deodorant pad is supposed to work. It keeps falling out of my armpit by the third day.

The other one that's got me puzzled is the eighteen-hour bra; why is it called that? Now, you've all seen Jane Russell on television talking about the eighteen-hour bra. Although I'm not in the market for a bra, I am a curious fellow by nature. I'm just dying to know what happens to that bra after eighteen hours. They ought to tell us, so our imaginations don't run wild.

Let's consider the possibilities. Maybe, after eighteen hours, it explodes. Now, that could be rough on an ordinary woman, but on a full-figured girl, it could be dynamite. Or, maybe after eighteen hours, it disintegrates, or maybe it shrinks, or maybe it bursts into flames. Yes sir, there could be a hundred reasons they named it the eighteen-hour bra, but I'll be blamed if I know why they would want to advertise any of them on television.

It's a frightening thought, but Jane Russell could be on a suicide mission.

Rock-a-Bye

I have heard it said that rock music appeals to the savage instincts of those who listen to it. I guess that's true, 'cause when I hear those loud noises, I want to go up on the stage and hurt the musicians.

But I know I shouldn't feel that way, so I decided to try to become more tolerant by listening to rock music and getting more familiar with it.

I went to a little club that was featuring a group called Leonard Rolaids and the Belchers. The first song they did was a ballad called, "I'm Gonna Tear off Your Clothes When the Wolfsbane Is in Bloom." Then they brought out their girl singer; her name was Bambi Whinette. She did a protest song called, "If You Try to Make Me Register for the Draft, I'll Drink Crazy Glue Till I Die, Bossa Nova."

Now, I was handling all this really well, and was fast adjusting to the fact that nobody in the band had a forehead, when it happened. The guy at the next table, wearing a T-shirt that said, "Truman Capote for President," walked up and asked me to dance.

You know, it was a shame the music was so loud, because I don't believe Leonard Rolaids and the Belchers ever knew why I was throwing them through the window.

Commercial Education

I am of the opinion that you can learn more from your average thirty-second televison commercial than you can from your average, matchbook correspondence course. Let me give you an example of what I mean. I'll change the name of the product, so I don't get my pants sued off, but here's how it goes:

The commercial opens up with this fellow standing behind a washing machine, telling you about new and improved Crudo Washing Powder. At this point, he holds up a shirt and says, "We are going to do a test." Now, the shirt he is holding is a man's long-sleeve dress shirt, and on the pocket it's got this big glob of chocolate syrup that measures about six inches by six inches. Then the guy on television shows you the elbow of the same shirt, and it's got about a pint of ketchup on the elbow.

He then ties a knot in the elbow of the shirt where the ketchup is and washes the shirt. Well, when it comes out of the washing machine, sure enough, all the chocolate syrup is gone. Then he unties the knot, and lo and behold, all the ketchup washed out, too.

He smiles real big and says, "Dirt can't hide from intensified Crudo."

Now, what do we learn from this? We learn never, ever go to lunch with the guy who owned that shirt.

Off-Color Country

Now, I'm not a prude by any stretch of the imagination, and I can handle obscenity as well as the next guy. But I've got to tell you, I am shocked at the current state of country/western music.

At first it was only suggestive, like, "We've Never Been This Far Before." Remember that? Then it started to get nasty.

I heard one the other day called, "I Want to Kiss Your Truck." Now, you tell me that ain't kinky! Or the new one called, "Statutory Rape Ain't Bad for a Start." Now, I ask you, does that kind of trash have any place in country/western music? Yes sir, I'm absolutely outraged.

Can you imagine a song called, "I Want To Woo-Woo Your Neck?" Now, I'm not sure what that means, but it sounds dirty to me. Or how about this: "I Don't Know Where Your Tattoo Is, but I Can Find It Before Fred."

Yes sir, the pornographic country and western songs are taking over, and I have only one thing to say: Gene Autry, where are you, when we need you most?

Bulldog Drummond Could Have Whipped Billie Jack

Every time a Hollywood movie makes money these days, the producers immediately make a sequel, hoping to pick up a few more bucks using their tried-and-true formula.

First there was *Jaws*, then *Jaws II*. *Rocky*, then *Rocky II* and *III*. *Star Wars*, then its several sequels. *The Godfather*, and then *The Godfather, Part II*. And let's not forget *Billie Jack*. That was followed by *The Trial of Billie Jack*, then *Billie Jack Goes to Washington*, then *Billie Jack Buys a Yo-Yo*, and finally *Billie Jack Gets a Hickey From Gidget While He's Kicking a Conservative to Death*.

They're making more and more sequels that cost more and more money, but in my opinion, they're not getting any better. I long for the days of the good movie series. Do you remember the Bowery Boys and the East Side Kids? Same bunch, just different names. The leader of the gang was Leo Gorsey, and his number one, right-hand man was always Hunts Hall. I don't know how many movies they made about the Bowery Boys and the East Side Kids, but I enjoyed every one of them, and that's more than I can say for Billie Jack.

Do you remember that wonderful series about the Thin Man — a rich private detective named Nick Charles and his beautiful debutante wife, named Nora? Nick was played by William Powell, Nora by the beautiful Myrna Loy. There were only seven Thin Man pictures. Every one was a classic that left you feeling great when the villain was brought to justice.

How could anyone forget the great Sherlock Holmes movies, starring Basil Rathbone as Holmes and Nigel Bruce as Doctor Watson? And what can compare with those great Charlie Chan movies? Charlie could solve any crime that came along. He was aided by his number-one son, and a chauffeur named Birmingham Brown. You remember Birmingham Brown; he's the man who coined the phrase, "Feet, do your duty."

And let's not forget Tarzan, Hopalong Cassidy, the Durango Kid, and Red Rider, as well as Henry Aldridge, Francis the Talking Mule, and Bulldog Drummond.

No sirree, movie sequels are not better today; they just show more skin and cost more money.

Food – The Forbidden Fruit

White Bread – Long May She Wave

You know, there was a time in this great country when you could order a ham sandwich and know down deep in your heart that you were going to get that sandwich on white bread. You could assume that, 'cause this is America.

America — the home of Will Rogers, Groucho Marx, Franklin Delano Roosevelt, and Li'l Abner. America — the birthplace of apple pie, baseball, the A-model Ford, and white bread. But I'm here to tell you that a dark cloud has descended over this beautiful land.

Folks have started using strange, foreign-tasting bread on their sandwiches. We should let the record show clearly that Americans, I mean real Americans, eat white bread.

Rye should be used in whiskey, not in bread. Pumpernickel should be used for patching potholes. Whole wheat bread should be toasted and used as frisbees.

When I was out of town recently, I checked into a hotel and called for room service. I ordered a ham sandwich and a cup of coffee. The waiter brought it up.

I said, "What's this?" He said, "Ham on rye." I said, "I didn't want a ham on rye." The waiter said, "That's the only kind of ham sandwich we have." I said, "Rye bread tastes bad." He said, "Our chef doesn't like any bread except rye." I said, "Your chef ain't gonna eat this sandwich, and neither am I, 'cause rye bread tastes like somebody spilled kerosene on it."

The waiter was not a nice person, 'cause at that point he hit me in the face with a side-order of potato salad.

I learned one valuable lesson: Never check into a hotel anywhere until you find out if they serve white bread.

Fancy Lunches

I had a strange experience the other day. My beautiful wife, Diane, talked me into going to one of those fancy, little places for lunch. You know, one of those places that serves only lunch and caters to women.

I knew as soon as I saw the napkins that I had made a mistake. They were little ol' bitty things with pictures of baby ducks sewn all over them. Now, I'm as liberal as the next guy, but there just ain't no way on earth I'm gonna wipe my mouth with pictures of little baby ducks.

The soup of the day was lettuce soup. Just think about that for a minute — lettuce soup.

I was the only man in the place, but the ladies there all seemed to be very pleased. I could hear them using words like charming, quaint, and divine.

I was doing fine until our waiter came over. He said, "My name is Maurice, and I will be your waiter." I said, "I'm Ludlow, and I will be your customer." My wife kicked me under the table.

We gave Maurice our order, and he tiptoed off toward the kitchen. In a minute he came back with our bread. Now, bear in mind, up to this minute I was being a perfect gentleman, but the bread was more than I could take. I called Maurice back over and said, "Maurice, how come my roll is hollow?"

He said, "That's not a roll; that's a popover."

So I said, "O.K., buster, why don't you pop over to the kitchen and get me some cornbread, 'cause if I'd wanted to eat a hole, I would have ordered doughnuts."

I don't really understand why my wife got so upset, 'cause I never would have hit old Maurice, if he hadn't called me a barbarian.

Diet Foods

My doctor told me the other day that I should leave off starches, fried foods, fats, and anything else that tastes good. He suggested that I go to a health food store and buy groceries. I was reluctant, but I thought I would give it a shot.

I drove to a place that had a big sign outside that said, "Long Life Health Food Store." I went in, and there was a fellow behind the counter who was about six-foot-three and weighed about ninety pounds. He had a scraggly beard that had about twenty-five hairs in it. His eyes were sunk back in his head so far that there was a slight echo when you spoke to him. He was wearing jeans, flip-flops, and a T-shirt that advertised Ajax All-Natural Bumblebee Soup.

He looked up as I walked to the counter, smiled, and said, "How can I help you, O large one?" I said, "I'm not sure you can help me at all, O wormy merchant, but my doctor told me to shop here, so here goes. I would like some great northern beans."

He sneered and said, "Do you know what you can get with great northern beans?" I said, "Yeah, onions and cornbread, if you're lucky."

He said, "We don't sell that killer food here. Don't you know we are what we eat?" I said, "If you're what you eat, skinny, you need to be on a diet more than I do."

I left the store, but it was a good experience for me. I learned that day that some things are worth dying for, and great northern beans, onions, and cornbread are three of them.

Ode To Bread

My diet is now into its third week,
And my longing for something has hit its peak.
I don't crave booze, or pizza, or abalone;
I don't crave cheese, or grits, or bologna.
I don't want apples, or oranges, or peaches,
'Cause they don't come close to where my craving reaches.
I have no desire for what ole McDonald sells,
And I wouldn't be caught where the Colonel dwells.
My craving, you see, has passed all bounds,
But I still don't want Tootsie Rolls or Mounds.
You see, dear hearts, after all is said,
I want only one thing, and that thing is *bread*.
I really don't care in what form it's presented,
But let me explain, if you think I'm demented.
I've loved bread since way back in my youth,
But let me tell you, so you'll know it's the truth.
When it comes to bread, I don't cull any,
And for a piece right now, I'd give my last penny.
Oh! Once again to gaze on a roll,
But don't go away, my story's not told.
I would never complain, not a word would I utter,
Especially if that roll was covered with butter.
Alas, to diet seems to be my fate, old friend,
So I'll stay with this diet to the bitter end.
I'll make my waist small, at last so be it,
I'm Ludlow Porch, and that's the way I see it.

Wonderful Grits

I fancy myself an unofficial spokesman for grits. Ahhh, wonderful grits! The most maligned of all delicacies. A wonderful versatile way to start your day.

There are many ways to fix grits; there are garlic grits, cheese grits, bacon grits, and many more. For my northern friends, I am going to tell you how to eat grits, because most northerners know very little about this Epicurean delight.

The thing that most northerners don't understand is that grits require a lot of preparing *after* they are on your plate. First, you add plenty of salt, and then you start with the black pepper. When you put so much pepper on your grits that you can hardly tell they were ever white, they are just about ready to eat.

Then you put a large dob of cow butter right in the middle of your hot grits. As the cow butter starts to melt, mix the salted and peppered grits with the melted butter, and then get ready for something good to eat.

Now, I don't believe in making brash statements, but I just bet when my northern friends try grits this way, they'll be sorry they won that war.

Those Little Onion Sandwiches

The older I get, the more I believe that progress is going to be the death of us all. Every time somebody wants to slide something by you, be it a tax increase or a land grab, they simply call it progress, and that seems to make it all right.

I have reached the point where I think progress is a buzz word; it really means, "Stand by, big boy, here it comes!" A perfect case in point is fast-food restaurants. The food at one time may have been fast, but the simple fact of the matter is that they ain't never been restaurants. Hamburger joints, maybe, but restaurants, never.

I grew up eating at one of those hamburger joints. The burgers were never much to write home about — small with more onion than beef. In fact, we called them little onion sandwiches. But they were cheap, and the service was quick, and that's the only reasons you went there in the first place. Well, bless Pat, along comes progress, and the whole onion sandwich empire is hanging by a thread.

When they added fried chicken to their menus, I didn't say a word. What the heck; I like chicken, and without some competition, the Colonel could very well get arrogant. But I noticed that after they added chicken to the menu, the service got slower.

Then they added drive-in windows, fancy uniforms, and started making expensive TV commercials. I thought, boy howdy, they're sure spending a lot of money just to sell those little onion sandwiches.

Then a few weeks ago, they finally managed to run me away forever.

I pulled up to the drive-in window, and a voice with a sissy French accent came over the speaker system. "My name is Pierre Lapew. How may I serve you?"

I said, "Give me eight with cheese, two fries, and two Cokes."

He answered, "Surely you jest."

I said, "Do what?"

"Our special of the day," he replied, "is chateaubriand for two — a mere fifty-six dollars."

"Do you have hamburgers?" I asked.

"Yes, we have hamburgers, but it will be a forty-minute wait. Or, if you like, we can mail them to you."

Well, that's progress for you. It got the dinosaur, and it's about got them little onion sandwiches.

While We Slept

Well, America, it has finally happened. While this great country slept, while we were distracted with such mundane matters as the SALT talks, the elections, and the President's domestic policy, it happened.

It happened while Rula Lenska smiled and told us about her hair spray. It happened while we were worrying about Arab oil, ERA, and gun control. I don't know who's to blame — the communists, the Democrats, the Republicans, the liberals, the conservatives. But I don't guess trying to place the blame is important.

What happened? Well, it grieves me to talk about it, but you have a right to know: The mashed potato, as we know it, is gone.

As an American, I guess I should feel angry at the passing of the mashed potato, but somehow I just feel sad. No matter what type of restaurant you go into now, you can't get real mashed potatoes, only instant mashed potatoes.

So, let this be our farewell to mashed potatoes, 'cause somewhere men are laughing and children shout. But there is no joy in my heart, since some yo-yo found out that you could put mashed potatoes in a box.

Look out, fried chicken, you'll be next.

Recipes

In another of my endless attempts to keep the public educated, I am about to share with you some of my most treasured recipes. As you read them, remember that these are some of the recipes which made me what I am today.

Ludlow's Recipe for Sunday Brunch

As soon as you're able to find the kitchen, put a pot of coffee on.

Chop an onion. (Anytime I go into the kitchen to cook a meal, I chop an onion. I'm bound to need it.)

Get out three skillets. One of them must be black. If you don't have a black skillet, go back to step one, drink the coffee, take a shower, and go have brunch at the Hilton. (You know, that ain't a bad idea, even if you have the skillet.)

Put a big spoonful of bacon grease in the black skillet, melt it, and turn off the heat. Put the onion in it.

Call a few children. (If you happen to be caught a little short in the children department, do all the work yourself and count your blessings.) One sets the table, one makes the orange juice, and one brings in the newspaper.

Sit down and drink some coffee and read a little of the paper.

Get a few baked potatoes out of the refrigerator, peel and chop them, and put them in the cold skillet with the onion. Salt and pepper them. (If you're not the type who has a few extra baked potatoes lying around, have grits. Of course, then you're going to have that greasy skillet and those soggy onions left. Too bad. You must learn to be more responsible.)

Now lay out the bacon in one skillet, and put the country ham in the other. Cover the country ham with water and *do not* turn on the stove. Go ahead and start the bacon. When you turn the bacon, pour off the water that's on the ham.

Turn the potatoes on medium high, and don't stir them much. Let them burn a little.

Preheat the oven to 400°.

Have the least messy of the children break about eight eggs into a bowl (or more, dogs love scrambled eggs). Add to that three slices of Old English cheese, torn into little pieces; two dashes of garlic powder; a bit of chopped parsley; and salt and pepper.

Turn the bacon again, and take a look at the potatoes and the ham.

Call the table-setter and remind him about the napkins. Have him put out the cream and sugar, butter and jelly, and salt and pepper.

Do something about the biscuits. I keep a batch in the freezer, but you may like canned ones, or you may want to whip up a batch fresh. (On Sunday? Really!) Whatever, do it now.

Have the brightest child slice the tomatoes and cantaloupe. *Do not* substitute another child. Even though the emergency rooms are not crowded during this time, it could put a damper on the day.

The bacon is burning!

Take up the bacon and the ham. Flip the potatoes over. More salt and pepper. Pour nearly all of the bacon grease into whatever you put bacon grease in.

Put the eggs into the bacon skillet. Turn them on medium-low.

Have the bright child pour coffee and juice. Tell the table-setter again about the napkins.

Stir the eggs, constantly scraping the bottom.

Go answer the phone.

Hurry back to the eggs. Cook until they're set.

Take out the biscuits, dish up the potatoes, get it all on the table.

Say the blessing.

Get up and go get the napkins.

Cornbread

It is very important that you use real bacon grease in this recipe. If you don't know how to get real bacon grease, don't worry about it, 'cause you probably wouldn't like the cornbread, anyway.

Ingredients:
2 cups self-rising cornmeal
1 egg
1¼ cups milk
2 Tbl. bacon grease, melted

Directions:

Preheat oven to 425°. Mix all ingredients. Pour into 8-inch, greased, square pan or skillet. (If you pour batter into a hot pan, it won't stick.) Bake 20 minutes.

Ludlow's Last Lick:

You have probably noticed, in other cookbooks, that sugar is called for. Anybody who would put sugar in cornbread is not right with the Lord, and don't know nothin' about eating in general and eating cornbread in particular.

Easy Chili

This chili is so authentic that after two bowls, you start to listen to Desi Arnaz records and spend days at a time watching "Cisco Kid" re-runs. In extreme cases, you try and sell your teen-aged sister to a member of the Armed Forces.

Ingredients:
butter to sauté
2 medium onions, chopped
1 lb. hamburger, lean
2 cans tomato sauce
2 cans Gebhardt Chili Beans
2 Tbl. chili powder
1 tsp. garlic powder

Directions:
Sauté onions. Add hamburger and brown. Drain well. Add other ingredients. Simmer, the longer, the better.

Hurry-Up Breakfast

This looks just awful on the plate, but don't worry about that, 'cause it tastes so good that after one bite, your eyes will roll back in your head so far you won't be able to see what you're eating, anyway.

Ingredients:
4 slices Canadian bacon
2 slices Swiss cheese, cut into halves
4 eggs
salt
pepper
¼ cup sour cream

Directions:

Preheat oven to 400°. Put bacon in bottom of an 8-inch pie pan. Put cheese over bacon. Break eggs over cheese. Sprinkle with salt and pepper. Spoon sour cream over eggs. Bake 15-20 minutes, while you take your shower.

Liver and Onions

You will notice that this book has no recipes for any kind of beef liver. The very best liver you can prepare ain't fit to eat, but, if you're just bent on eating liver, this is less offensive than most.

Frankly, I think you'd enjoy a cheese sandwich more, but suit yourself.

Ingredients:
chicken livers
½ cup butter or margarine
3 medium onions, cut into rings
Worcestershire sauce, to taste

Directions:

Melt butter in a big iron skillet over medium heat. Put in livers and scatter onion rings over them. Dribble the Worcestershire sauce over top and cover skillet. Peek in now and then, and, when they are less disgusting to look at, remove the cover. Stir now and then till they look done.

Pimento Cheese

If you're going to have pimento cheese, you must make it yourself. People who eat store-bought pimento cheese tend to be criminals and keep pictures of known communists in their billfolds.

Ingredients:
sharp Cheddar cheese, grated
mayonnaise, to moisten
pimentos
onion, finely chopped

Directions:
Mix and eat.

Ludlow's Last Lick:
The onion is the secret here, but use only a tiny amount. And *don't* store it with the onion in it.

Irish Coffee

One cup is very enjoyable.
Two cups will make you warm all over.
Three cups will make your knees not work.
Four cups will make you drunk.
Five cups will make you think you're a spare tire from a '48 Studebaker.

Ingredients for each drink:
¼ cup Irish whiskey
1 tsp. vanilla flavoring
2 Tbl. brown sugar
coffee
Cool Whip (frozen)

Directions:
Into each mug, pour whiskey, vanilla flavoring, and brown sugar. Add coffee. Top with frozen Cool Whip.

Ludlow's Last Lick:
Irish Coffee can be improved, if you'll add about one "glug" of Tia Maria to each cup.

Sue's Little Chicken Sandwiches

When you first see these darling little sandwiches, you're gonna think that they look like something sissies eat. Don't let that stop you. They're delicious, and you'll be surprised how seven or eight of them will fill you up.

Ingredients:
1 lb. cream cheese, softened
½ cup Miracle Whip Salad Dressing (must use this brand)
5 oz. canned boneless chicken
5 bacon slices, cooked crisp and crumbled
5 green onions
bread

Directions:

Mix cream cheese and salad dressing well. Add the remaining ingredients (except bread) and stir gently with a fork until well blended. Chill. Cut crusts from bread and spread with chicken mixture. If you plan to hold them for awhile, cover them with damp paper towels and keep in the refrigerator.

Ludlow's Last Lick:

Be sure to remove the paper towels before you eat the sandwiches, if you don't want them to taste like the Quicker Picker-Upper.

And if you are ever invited to my cousin Sue's, *go*. Sue can whup some food on you!

Vichyssoise

Don't let the name of this fool you, 'cause it ain't nothing on earth but cold 'tater soup, and the very best you ever put into your mouth. I like to put it in a cup and sip on it while watching TV. My wife says that's part of my cotton mill background. She may be right, but it sure tastes good that way.

Ingredients:
3 leeks
2 Tbl. butter
1 small onion, sliced
3 cups chicken broth (or half broth and half water)
2 tsp. salt
4 medium potatoes, peeled and sliced
1½ cups milk
1½ cups half-and-half
¾ cup whipping cream
chives, chopped, for garnish

Directions:

Wash leeks and remove roots and green tops. Melt butter in large pot. Add leeks and onion. Cook till limp. (If needed, add more butter.) Heat chicken broth and salt. Add potatoes. Bring to a boil and simmer 40 minutes, or until potatoes are tender. Pour into food processor or blender and process until completely smooth. Return to pot and add milk and half-and-half. Bring it just to the boiling point, but do *not* boil.

Cool mixture. Run through a fine strainer. (If you're just not up to that, run it through the processor again.) When soup is cold, add whipping cream. This will need about four hours in the refrigerator to get cold. Serve topped with chives.

Boo-Boo's Creole Red Beans and Rice

You will notice, as you read this, that Boo-Boo says it will serve twelve people. The fact of the matter is that it will serve twenty very large men who just escaped from a P.O.W. camp.

Ingredients for 12 servings:
2 lbs. dried red kidney beans
water to soak in
2 medium yellow onions, chopped
3 or 4 ham hock "chunks"
2-3 lbs. smoked pork sausage, cut into 1-inch slices, uncooked
3 Tbl. salt
1 Tbl. black pepper
1 Tbl. cayenne pepper
water to cook in
2-3 quarts white rice, cooked

Directions:

Place dried kidney beans in large Dutch oven. Add water until the water is four inches above the beans. Cover, let soak overnight. Drain onion, ham hocks, sausage, and spices. Add just enough water to completely cover ingredients. Stir well. Cook for 3 hours over low to medium heat, stirring every 20 minutes or so. After 3 hours, beans should be quite tender. Remove ¾ cup of beans, mash them thoroughly and return to mixture. Cook 30 minutes more. Serve over rice with hot French bread.

Ludlow's Last Lick:

A honey-baked ham bone added to the meat ingredients is great! Any ham bone is good, for that matter. Use a high-quality, name-brand sausage. Always use old-fashioned, raw, long-grain rice that you cook from scratch.

Broccoli Casserole

I'm not big on broccoli. If the Lord had wanted us to eat broccoli, he would not have invented turnip greens. But this recipe has enough Cheddar cheese and onions in it to overpower the broccoli taste and make it taste really good. Even kids will love it.

Ingredients:
2 packages chopped frozen broccoli
1 can cream of celery soup
1 onion, chopped
½ cup Cheddar cheese, diced
1 can fried onions

Directions:

Cook broccoli according to package directions. Drain. Add remaining ingredients (except fried onions). Bake, uncovered, at 350° until bubbly. Sprinkle onions on top, and bake another minute or so.

Boo-Boo's Cajun Seafood Gumbo

This recipe will require taking out a second mortgage on your house or canceling your child's college plans, but I think it's worth it.

Ingredients for serving an army:
¾ cup salad oil
1 cup flour
3 large yellow onions, chopped
6 stalks celery, cleaned and chopped
1 bell pepper, cleaned and chopped
4 cloves garlic, minced
1 quart water, warm
4 Tbl. salt
2 Tbl. black pepper
1 Tbl. cayenne pepper
2 Tbl. Worcestershire sauce (Lea and Perrin's is strongly recommended)
2 bay leaves
5 quarts water
1 can Ro-Tel tomatoes with chili peppers
1 lb. "lump" crab meat
2 10-oz. package of sliced frozen okra, cooked according to package directions
2 lbs. medium-sized shrimp, cleaned and de-veined
1 dozen whole, cleaned crabs (including claws)
1 pint oysters, drained (optional)
⅓ cup green onion tops, chopped
¼ cup *fresh* parsley, minced
white rice, cooked
filé to garnish

Directions:

Make a roux (pronounced "rew") with the oil and flour as follows: Heat oil in large, heavy Dutch oven for 3 minutes over medium-high heat. Gradually add flour, stirring constantly. Continue cooking for 4-5 minutes. Reduce heat to medium. Continue cooking 15-20 minutes, stirring constantly (scrape bottom and sides of pot vigorously). The mixture will turn from a very light brown to a murky brown color, developing a strong aroma as it darkens. *This point is critical*. The roux will continue to darken quickly. It is done when it is the color of a Hershey bar, although it will have a slightly reddish hue. This is a long, hot process, as the roux burns very easily, but it is the key to a successful gumbo.

Add onions, celery, bell pepper, and garlic to the roux. Stir constantly over medium heat 15 minutes. The mixture will turn almost black, and the oil will tend to separate from the mixture slightly.

Gradually add warm water to the mix. It will turn from near-black to medium brown, as you do so. Add salt, peppers, and Worcestershire sauce. Stir well. Cook over medium heat for 15 minutes.

Add 5 quarts water, tomatoes, crab meat, and okra. Stir well, reduce heat to medium-low, and cook 2 hours, stirring occasionally.

Add shrimp, whole crabs, crab claws, and oysters (if desired). Simmer over low-medium heat 30 minutes. Skim off foam.

Turn off heat, add onion tops and parsley. Stir well.

Serve over rice; garnish with filé (pronounced "fee-lay").

Ludlow's Last Licks:

The roux is the key ingredient. It takes patience. I can't overemphasize the need to stir and scrape constantly, until the roux is done. *Never* put the filé in the gumbo while cooking. This freezes beautifully, unless you use the oysters. Serve with potato salad, hot French bread, and white wine on a cold, crisp night.

Chicken Salad

This is what I call drugstore chicken salad, because it tastes just like the delicious chicken salad you used to be able to buy at the drugstore.

If you want something good, toast two pieces of Colonial bread, spread a generous portion of chicken salad on the bread, get you a cherry Coke, sit under an overhead fan, and listen to Glenn Miller records.

Precious memories — how they linger!

Ingredients:
chicken breasts, boiled, cooled, and diced
mayonnaise, to moisten
celery
salt
pepper

Directions:

Add enough mayonnaise to moisten chicken. Add celery, salt, and pepper to taste.

Cocktail Meatballs

Be sure to fix plenty of these, 'cause sooner or later, you're gonna have some of your white-trash friends over, and they're gonna eat these like they were going to the chair.

Ingredients:
1 lb. lean ground beef
¾ cup wheat germ
1 medium onion, chopped
1 egg, lightly beaten
salt
pepper
garlic powder
Sauce:
1 12-oz. bottle of chili sauce
1 10-oz. jar grape jelly
juice of 1 lemon

Directions:

Mix all ingredients (except for sauce) thoroughly and form into bite-sized balls. Mix all sauce ingredients in a large pot. Add meatballs to sauce and simmer 30 minutes, stirring occasionally. When the meatballs are done, reserve the sauce and serve the meatballs in a chafing dish. I usually make a new batch of sauce to pour over them.

Ludlow's Favorite Potato Recipe

This is the best way on earth to eat a potato. If you don't like these, you're probably too close to death to care much about food. I would, therefore, suggest that you close this book at once and seek medical help.

Ingredients:
potatoes, raw
butter
oil

Directions:

Cut potatoes into halves and scoop out balls with melon ball cutter. (I use the large end.) Cook *very* slowly in an iron skillet with lots of butter and a little oil. Don't cover the potato balls with the butter, about half-covered will do. Cook until golden. There's a lot of wasted potato with this, but it's worth it.

Mother's Smothered Chicken

Ingredients:

5 or 6 chicken breasts
1 cup flour
1 Tbl. salt
½ tsp. pepper
oil
3½ cups milk

Directions:

Clean chicken and remove skin. Roll chicken in flour mixed with salt and pepper. Heat the oil until it is hot, but not smoking. Brown chicken and remove from pan. Pour off all but 4 Tbl. oil. Return pan to medium heat and stir in ¼ cup of the remaining flour mixture. Cook 60 seconds, stirring constantly. Keep stirring, and add the milk very slowly. Heat to boiling. Return chicken to pan. Simmer 1½ hours. Stir now and then, and if it starts getting too thick, add a little more milk. Taste and correct seasonings.

Ludlow's Mama's Last Lick:

When I ask Ludlow if he would like Smothered Chicken for supper, he always says, "No, kill it the regular way." It just goes to prove, you can't be funny *all* the time.

Shrimp Salad

If you have a few extra dollars, you should hire somebody to peel and clean the shrimp. If you can't afford it, then I wouldn't fool with this. Speaking for myself, this recipe calls for a much closer relationship than I care to have with shrimp.

Ingredients:
shrimp, cleaned, boiled, and cut into small pieces
celery
mayonnaise, to moisten
salt
pepper
juice from ½ lemon

Directions:

Use two parts shrimp to one part celery. Add celery to shrimp. Moisten with mayonnaise. Add remaining ingredients. Chill well.

Ludlow's Last Lick:

Put it in a sandwich with lettuce, stuff a tomato with it, or just eat it straight out of the refrigerator.

Strawberry Pie

This pie is *not* for folks on a diet. I gained seven pounds just typing this.

Ingredients:
1 3¾-oz. package vanilla pudding and pie filling mix
1 baked 10-inch pie shell, cooled
8 ladyfingers, split
1 pint strawberries
1 jar red currant jelly
2 tsp. water
whipped cream for garnish

Directions:

Prepare pie filling as directed on the box. Cool it for 5 minutes, stirring now and then to prevent skin from forming. Pour filling into the pie shell. Cool to room temperature. Cover filling with ladyfingers, cut side down. Hull strawberries and cut in two. Arrange berry halves, cut side down, in circles over ladyfingers. Place them very close together. Heat jelly and water until melted and smooth. Cool. Spoon over berries. Chill several hours. Just before serving, garnish with whipped cream around the border.

Spaghetti Sauce

Ingredients:

2 medium onions, chopped
2 cloves garlic, minced
½ lb. mushrooms
1 lb. lean ground beef
1 can stewed tomatoes
2 cans tomato sauce
1 can tomato paste (optional)
¼ cup Worcestershire sauce
1 Tbl. oregano
1 Tbl. sugar
1 tsp. salt
1 tsp. pepper
1 tsp. garlic powder
Parmesan cheese, grated

Directions:

Sauté onions and garlic until translucent. Add mushrooms. Cook until tender. Add ground beef. Cover. Cook until done, stirring occasionally. Drain well. Add remaining ingredients. Simmer an hour. Serve over thin spaghetti. Sprinkle with Parmesan cheese. *Fresh* Parmesan cheese that you grate yourself makes all the difference.

Ludlow's Last Lick:

The only way you can improve on this spaghetti, is to eat it with garlic bread, then lay down and sleep for about eight days.

Spinach-Artichoke Business (Dedicated to Miss Diane)

This is not one of my personal favorites, but Boo-Boo really loves it. You should bear in mind, however, that Boo-Boo will eat an end table.

Ingredients for 8 servings:
¼ lb. butter (*not* margarine)
2 medium yellow onions, chopped
4 10-oz. boxes frozen chopped spinach, cooked and drained
1 pint sour cream
½ cup Parmesan cheese
2 16-oz. cans artichoke hearts, drained
⅔ cup Progresso seasoned bread crumbs
2 Tbl. salt
1 Tbl. black pepper
⅓ cup Progresso bread crumbs
⅛ lb. butter (*not* margarine)

Directions:

Melt ¼ lb. butter in a 4-quart Dutch oven. Sauté onions 10 minutes. Add spinach, sour cream, Parmesan cheese, salt, pepper, and ⅔ cup bread crumbs. Mix thoroughly. Gently fold in artichoke hearts till evenly distributed. Turn off heat. Pour mixture into shallow, 3-quart casserole. Sprinkle ⅓ cup bread crumbs over mixture. Slice ⅛ lb. butter into ¼-inch pats. Place evenly over bread crumbs. Bake at 350° for 30 minutes.

Ludlow's Last Lick:

Use a well-known brand of spinach, not the house brand (I use Bird's Eye brand). I also highly recommend Progresso brand artichoke hearts, where they are available.

*Best Friend** Chicken Casserole

Ingredients:

1 large fryer (or 5 chicken breasts)
¼ lb. margarine
1½ cups chicken broth (reserved from boiling chicken)
1 can cream of celery soup
1 can cream of chicken soup
1 soup can of whole milk
1 package cornbread stuffing mix

Directions:

Boil chicken until tender. Reserve broth. Skin and cut chicken into small pieces. Place in the bottom of a 9-inch-by-13-inch casserole. Melt margarine in the broth, while the broth is still hot. Mix soups and milk together and pour over diced chicken. Sprinkle stuffing mix over soups. Just before you put casserole in oven, pour broth over stuffing. Bake 1 hour at 350°.

Ludlow's Last Lick:

Even if you aren't hungry, make this. It makes the house smell terrific.

*The Best Friend is Judy Merritt; Perry, Georgia's finest.

Milky Way Cake

There are no words to describe this dessert.

Ingredients:
6 1-oz. Milky Way bars
½ cup butter or margarine
2 cups sugar
1 cup shortening
4 eggs
2½ cups flour
1 tsp. salt
1½ cups buttermilk
½ tsp. soda
1 tsp. vanilla flavoring

Directions:

Combine candy bars and butter in a heavy saucepan over low heat, stirring constantly until melted. Cream sugar and shortening. Add eggs, beating until light and creamy. Combine flour and salt. Combine buttermilk and soda. Alternately add dry ingredients and buttermilk mixture to creamed mix, beating well after each addition. Stir in candy bar mixture and vanilla flavoring. Pour batter into 3 greased and floured 9-inch cake pans. Bake at 350° 30 minutes, or until done.

When layers are completely cool, frost with Chocolate Marshmallow Frosting.

Chocolate-Marshmallow Frosting

Ingredients:

2 cups sugar
1 13-oz. can evaporated milk
½ cup butter or margarine
1 6-oz. package semisweet chocolate chips
1 cup marshmallow cream

Directions:

Mix sugar, milk, and butter in heavy saucepan. Cook over medium heat, until a small amount dropped in cold water forms a soft ball.

Remove from heat. Add chocolate pieces and marshmallow cream. Stir until melted.

Aunt Barbara's Rice

Ingredients:

¼ lb. butter or margarine, melted
1 medium onion, chopped
¼ cup rice, uncooked
1 can Campbell's Beef Consommé
1 can water
2 beef bullion cubes

Directions:

Pour butter into a 2-quart casserole. Add rice and consummé. Boil water. Dissolve bullion cubes in boiling water. Pour into casserole. Cover and bake at 350° for 30-45 minutes.

Ludlow's Last Lick:

This is one of those great recipes you can fix ahead of time and then bake when the roast is about ready. And if you think this is good, you should try Aunt Barbara's squash!

Aunt Teenie's Pepper Relish

Ingredients:

12 green peppers, chopped
12 red peppers, chopped
12 medium onions, chopped
boiling water to cover
2 cups sugar
2 cups vinegar
3 Tbl. salt
water, boiling

Directions:

Cover peppers and onions with boiling water and let stand 5 minutes. Drain. Add remaining ingredients (except boiling water) and boil 5 minutes. Pour into 8 hot 1-pint jars. Process 5 minutes in a boiling water bath, to insure that jars are properly sealed. Serve this relish with fresh vegetables or eat it right out of the jar.

Ludlow's Last Lick:

The water bath is very important. If you try to do this in the shower, it makes the relish taste soapy.

Aunt Teenie uses a knife to chop the peppers evenly, but if you're lazy and care only about taste, go on and use the food processor. It's still wonderful.

Trivial Trivia

Ludlow's Trivia Quiz

1. What was Burt Reynolds' name on "Gunsmoke?"
2. Who was the co-pilot in *The High and Mighty*?
3. What was the last line of *True Grit*?
4. In what movie did Bogart say, "Play it again, Sam?"
5. Who wrote "Gunga Din?"
6. Who were the announcers on "Burns and Allen?"
7. Who was Steve Allen's announcer on "The Tonight Show?"
8. What was Doctor Joyce Brothers' category on "The $64,000 Question?"
9. Name Buddy Hackett's television series.
10. Who was Horace McNalley?
11. Who wrote *Treadmill to Oblivion*?
12. Who played the original Trader Horn?
13. Name the Ida Lupino-Howard Duff series.
14. Who was Rod Redwing?
15. Who was heavyweight champion before Joe Louis?
16. On TV, who was "brave, courageous, and true?"
17. Who said, "We'll go on forever, 'cause we're the people?"
18. Who was the fictional hero of *The Maltese Falcon*?
19. What is Sugar Ray Robinson's real name?
20. Who was Jack Parr's band leader?
21. Name Long John Silver's parrot.
22. What kind of bird delivered Groucho's secret word?
23. Who was the radio sponsor of "Your Hit Parade?"
24. Name Kay Kyser's radio show.
25. Who sponsored the Ames Brothers' TV show?
26. Who coached Davis and Blanchard at West Point?
27. Who coached Jim Thorpe at Carlisle?
28. What was Mike Barnett against?
29. Who starred in *Dear Phoebe*?
30. Who was the monkey on "The Today Show?"

31. Name the night club in *Casablanca*.
32. Allen Hale, Jr., has had two series. Name them.
33. Who was host of "Welcome, Traveler."
34. Name the ranch in *Red River*.
35. Who was the star of *Our American Cousin* the night Lincoln was shot?
36. Name Donald Duck's nephews.
37. Name Mickey Mouse's nephews.
39. Where did Steve Wilson work?
40. What was Mr. Belvedere's first name?
41. What was John Wayne's name in *Sands of Iwo Jima*?
42. Who played the title role in *The Stratton Story*?
43. What was the question that Jack Bailey asked every day on "Queen for a Day?"
44. Who was the "Queen of the Golden West?"
45. What was Sky King's airplane's name?
46. Who played the Durango Kid?
47. Who was George Gobel's TV wife?
48. Who was his girl singer?
49. What was the name of Arthur Murray's TV Show?
50. Who led three lives?
51. What singing group was featured on Bob Crosby's TV show?
52. Who said, "Nothing is so exhilarating as to be shot at without result?"
53. What was Peter Lorre's name in *The Maltese Falcon*?
54. What movie introduced Ma and Pa Kettle?
55. Who was Margaret Dumont?
56. Who was Andy Hardy's girlfriend?
57. Who played Henry Aldrich in the movies?
58. What is the full name of the Phantom's girlfriend?
59. Who played the albino in *God's Little Acre*?
60. What is Evel Knievel's first name?

61. What was the name of the taxi company on "Amos 'n' Andy?"
62. Who played Mr. Miniver?
63. Who was Teddy Nadler?
64. What was Jesse James' wife's name?
65. What was Hot-Shot Charlie's full name?
66. Where was "The Heartbreak Hotel?"

Answers to Ludlow's Trivia Quiz

1. Quint Asper
2. John Wayne
3. "Come see a fat, old man, sometimes."
4. He never said it.
5. Rudyard Kipling
6. Harry Von Zell
7. Gene Rayburn
8. Boxing
9. "Stanley"
10. Stephen McNally's real name is Horace.
11. Fred Allen
12. Harry Carey, Sr.
13. "Mr. Adams and Eve"
14. He taught most Hollywood cowboys the fast draw.
15. Jim Braddock
16. Wyatt Earp
17. Ma Joad
18. Sam Spade
19. Walker Smith
20. Jose Melis
21. Captain Flint
22. A duck
23. Lucky Strike Cigarettes
24. "Kay Kyser Kollege of Musical Knowledge"

25. R.C. Cola
26. Red Blake
27. Pop Warner
28. Crime ("Man Against Crime")
29. Peter Lawford
30. J. Fred Muggs
31. Rick's Café American
32. "Casey Jones" and "Gilligan's Island"
33. Tommy Bartlett
34. The Red River D
35. Laura Keane
36. Huey, Dewey, and Louie
37. Morty and Ferdie
39. *The Illustrated Press*
40. Lynn
41. John Stryker
42. Jimmy Stewart
43. "Would you like to be queen for a day?"
44. Dale Evans
45. The Songbird
46. Charles Starret
47. Alice, played by Jeff Dunnell
48. Pretty, perky Peggy King
49. "Arthur Murray's Dance Party"
50. Herbert Philbrick
51. The Modernaires
52. Winston Churchill
53. Joel Cairo
54. *The Egg and I*
55. The foil of the Marx Brothers
56. Polly Benedict
57. Jimmy Lydon

58. Diana Palmer
59. Michael Landon
60. Robert
61. Fresh Air Taxi Company
62. Greer Garson
63. Big winner on several quiz shows in the fifties
64. Zee
65. Charles C. Charles
66. Down at the end of Lonely Street